The Goddess Journaling Workbook

*365 daily journaling prompts
to keep a manifestation mindset all year round*

by Beatrix Minerva Linden

To the future, better versions of ourselves,
who exist somewhere,
waiting to be risen
from our very own Underworlds.

The Goddess Journaling Workbook
Copyright © 2019 Beatrix Minerva Linden
All rights reserved. Independent publication.

ISBN: 9781696918237

Disclaimer: no part of this book can be copied nor reproduced without previous consent. We want to express our sincere thanks to the independent artists who created the fonts Homemade Text and Husna, which have been used for titles throughout the book. Cover images credits: Depositphotos. This book is not meant to cure nor diagnose any ailments and it does not substitute the advice of a doctor or a therapist. People with prior issues, especially past trauma, mental health issues, PTSD, etc., are advised to ask their doctor or therapist before they start journaling. All the information in this book is given subjectively and exclusively for entertainment purposes; if you decide to follow the journaling program presented in this book, please understand that you do it solely under your own responsibility. The author gives you no warranty of achieving your intended results. An effort was made to ensure the information offered was correct at the time of writing, but the author doesn't assume any liabilities for any troubles or losses caused by errors or omissions in this publication. Thanks for reading.

INTRODUCTION

What is *The Goddess Journaling Workbook*?

This is a book to help you start journaling and remain in a manifestation mindset for a whole year. The workbook is not dated, so you can start writing anytime. You will need <u>five to ten minutes per day</u>, but if you stick to doing it consistently, <u>you will be able to create a journaling habit which can last a lifetime.</u>

Using this journal is extremely easy: it is structured in **six cycles, each of them represented by one Greek Goddess**, who embodies the goals we will work on during that cycle. <u>The writing prompts use manifestation principles</u> and the law of attraction. This way, journaling becomes much more than a comforting habit: it can help you define your dreams clearly and find a way to achieve them.

How to work with this journal

There are six cycles in this journal. **<u>They all start with a brief passage about a Greek Goddess and how you can use her energy in your life</u>**. The first Goddess in this workbook is Persephone, the Queen of the Underworld: you will soon discover why. Her energy will accompany you for your first eight weeks of journaling.

<u>After that, you can go straight to Day 1.</u> All days follow the same structure, although the tasks and writing prompts may vary:

- **<u>Daily positive affirmations:</u>** you can read the affirmations in the morning: for example, as soon as you wake up, while having breakfast or commuting. <u>It will take you less than two minutes</u>. There is a different affirmation for every day of the year. Try to keep the daily affirmation in mind throughout the day. A good way to do so is to re-read it often or write it down on a visible place (for example, you can write it on a sticky note and put it on your computer screen, refrigerator, or even on the back of your phone). Meditate about the daily affirmation and believe it

can happen: try to visualize it happening and becoming true.
- **Journaling prompts to manifest your goals:** below the daily affirmations you will find a brief journaling prompt. Most journaling prompts take five minutes to complete. Some will require more thinking, while others can be answered with just one word. It doesn't matter how many lines you fill: it's the daily writing habit that counts.
- **Gratitude Journal:** imagine you were the parent of a spoiled child. Imagine yourself showering that child with presents, as he keeps complaining about all the toys he doesn't have yet, blind to everything he already has. Would you keep fulfilling that child's wishes? Or would you become angry at his ungratefulness and rather keep your presents for someone else? Manifestation principles work in a very similar way: the common belief is that in order for miracles to happen, we must start by feeling truly thankful for what we already have. Don't blind yourself with other people's possessions and achievements, thinking you are less lucky than they are. Focus on your own life, your own achievements, and all the things you *do* have and can be grateful for. Even on a really bad day we can be thankful for the air we breathe, the clothes keeping us warm and the fact that we are still alive and able to work for a better tomorrow.

The best moment to practice gratitude is in the evenings, ideally at the end of the day. Each day, write about something good which took place or you heard of. Write it down and feel *truly* thankful for it as you do it. It's possible to be thankful for really small events: catching the bus on time, reading some good news, or getting a kiss from your child are just a few of those little things which help remind us how lucky we already are.

Let the Goddesses guide your path

There are many people who still believe in the classical Gods and Goddesses, but you don't have to be one of them in order to use this workbook successfully. **You can understand the different Goddesses and their energies as metaphors or archetypes and use them as a source of journaling inspiration.** In this book we will work with feminine deities from the Greek and Roman pantheons. <u>Each of them has a specific realm of influence you can explore, as you dig into your inner world, expand your consciousness and plan for the life you wish to manifest.</u>

The stories of these Goddesses are meant to inspire you and guide you on your path towards personal transformation. During the following 365 days we will walk hand in hand with:

- *Goddess Persephone/Proserpine:* she will help you with introspection, as you travel through your very own Underworld;
- *Goddess Artemis/Diana*: she will help you discover your cycles, explore your most feminine side, and birth the new you;
- *Goddess Athena/Minerva*: with her help, you will collect the necessary knowledge to become who you want to be;
- *Goddess Aphrodite/Venus*: she will encourage you to love yourself and your body, and find the love you deserve;
- *Goddess Hestia/Vesta*: she will help you achieve home and family happiness and manifest material comfort;
- *Goddess Demeter/Ceres*: to finish the yearly cycle, Demeter will symbolize harvesting the fruits of your efforts, giving the final shape to your wishes and preparing for a new period of introspection.

I encourage you to keep researching about each Goddess during the eight weeks or so each journaling cycle lasts. Not all prompts will be directly related to each Goddess, because our goal is to encompass the many facets of life during each journaling cycle. You will find some Goddesses and their myths more appealing than others, and that's just normal. But still, let the power of all six Goddesses ignite the divine feminine in you and guide you, as you manifest the life of your dreams.

The benefits of journaling

Journaling has many benefits, such as:

- **Clearing up scattered minds**: journaling is ideal for busy workers, mothers of little children and actually anyone who has too much in their mind and on their shoulders, and needs an easy way to relax and center,

- **Meditating actively**: journaling can be considered active meditation, and so it is ideal for people who don't want to or can't meditate, because they are too active or fidgety, and they need to move or do something all the time. If you have trouble staying still and silent, or keeping your mind empty of thoughts for a whole meditation session, journaling can be a great substitute with comparable benefits.
- **Becoming more creative:** in the last years, there have been a few studies which proved that writing by hand helps people learn and remember things and have better ideas. There seems to be a connection between tracing letters by hand and activating certain parts of the brain which remain dormant or less stimulated when just reading or typing on a keyboard.[1]

The link between journaling and goal manifestation

Manifesting is just another way of saying *making our dreams come true*. We say something ***manifested*** when an object or situation which started as a thought in our mind became tangible and real. The first one to talk openly about the principles of manifestation seems to be an American clockmaker from the 1800's called Phineas Quimby, although the first one to name the **Law of Attraction** in a book was the Russian occultist Helena Blavatsky, in her 1877 esoteric book *Isis Unveiled*[2]. Since then, many others have written about possible ways to change our mindset in order to manifest our desires.

The first rule of manifestation is *keeping an optimistic attitude*. That's why we will start each day with positive affirmations. Secondly, it's quite logical that **you can't make your dreams come true if you don't know clearly what those dreams are.** Thoughts such as "*oh, I hate this job!*" are not going to take you very far:

---

[1] *The Wall Street Journal, www.wsj.com,* **How Handwriting Trains the Brain: Forming Letters Is Key to Learning, Memory, Ideas, Freedom and Discipline** *(Online, 2019)* and National Center for Biotechnology Information, www.ncbi.nlm.nih.gov, **The effects of handwriting experience on functional brain development in pre-literate children** *(Online, 2019)*

[2] *Wikipedia,* **Law of attraction (New Thought),** *(Online, September 2019) and The Theosophical Society of Pasadena, California, www.theosociety.org,* **Isis Unveiled — H. P. Blavatsky,** *(Online, 2019).*

but these are the ones which seem to repeat in our minds if we don't practice conscious **mind-gardening**. Manifestation requires that you formulate your wishes:

- As positive statements (*I want to be a dentist* vs *I hate this job*);
- In a very specific way (*I want to get a job as a hotel receptionist which pays at least 2000 per month* vs *I want a new job,* which is too vague);
- In a thankful way, and using the present tense when possible (*I am thankful for getting a job as a dentist*, etc.).

And this is where journaling can be of great help. Journaling helps enormously with manifestation because it:

- Clears up the clutter in your mind;
- Helps you see your true goals and wishes clearly;
- Helps you get to know yourself and your limitations better;
- Helps you define a realistic way to reach your goals,
- Helps you keep a calm state of mind which will also assist you in reaching your goals.

How to overcome the "*I have no time*" adage

The first thing you can remind yourself is that you don't need that much time for journaling. Even four minutes is infinitely better than zero. Think about things you can do in five minutes: wash your teeth, browse social media, or check your email. You probably do some of those things many times a day without a second thought.

This is not about writing *a lot*, but about writing *often*. The only important thing is finding time to write every day. Journaling is not like writing a novel: one word per day can be more than enough.

Be creative and find short periods of time in your day to day. Maybe you can journal while commuting, during your lunch break, while you wait for your kids or before you go to bed. You can even keep your journal next to the toilet, why not?

Frequency is much more important than quantity. It doesn't matter *how much* or *where* you write. The only important thing is to create a lifetime habit. If you are forgetful, set an alarm on your phone (or two, or three), until you get used to journaling every day.

What if I don't like a writing prompt or I find it repetitive?

It's your journal. Feel free to journal about something else if you want to. There may be subjects which you find more interesting and others which don't apply to you so much. There are themes which repeat themselves with different words or from different points of view: this is on purpose, because motivation is fueled by steadiness. There will be times when you will not feel like journaling about a subject because it makes you feel uncomfortable. In such cases, it's good to ask yourself *why*.

Finally, you can sign a contract with yourself, expressing your commitment to journaling for a certain period of time. You can fill it in in the following page.

A promise to myself:

*I promise myself to journal every day.
I'm committed to becoming a better version of myself,
so that I can manifest the life of my dreams.*

*Signed:*_____

*Date:*_____

Additional comments:

FIRST JOURNALING CYCLE

Goddess Persephone

Persephone is the Greek Goddess of innocence and the Queen of the Underworld. Take advantage of the first journaling cycle to pay a brief visit to your very own *Underworld*. The next eight weeks are a great opportunity to explore your past and make peace with your inner child, so you can start sowing the seeds of your new life on a clean, blank slate.

Goddess Persephone lives in the Underworld: at first she didn't want to, but after a while she learned to love the darkness as much as she loved the light. She represents the winter of our souls and the dark side we all possess. We need to embrace that darkness, forgive it and love it, so we can love and accept ourselves. If you love and appreciate yourself, you will be much more likely to keep the positive mindset necessary to achieve great things. There's nothing wrong with paying visits to the Underworld of our mind from time to time.[3]

Persephone's story

Persephone is also known as Proserpine in Roman mythology. She is the daughter of Demeter, the Goddess of harvest. One day, young Persephone was seen by Hades, the King of the Underworld, and he immediately fell in love with her. He took her to the Underworld against her will, and when she and her mother protested, the Gods decided to help her go back to the upper realm. But Hades pointed out that she had eaten a pomegranate during her stay in the Underworld. The pomegranate was considered the fruit of the dead, and anyone who ate it should remain in the Land of the Dead forever. But Demeter, Goddess of harvest and Persephone's mother, was so sad that she turned all the land barren with her grief. Finally, a consensus with Hades was achieved: Persephone would spend a few months per year as the Queen of the Underworld, but she would return every year to the upper realm to be with her

---

[3] *As stated before, people who have gone through past trauma and mental health issues might want to ask their doctors and therapists before they start journaling about past experiences.*

mother for a while. This cycle would repeat itself every year.

This agreement caused the land to go through the seasons of the year. While Persephone was in the Underworld, her mother Demeter was always extremely sad: that's why the land remained barren during the winter months. When Persephone came back to her mother every year, Demeter brought the spring to the world and everything started to blossom again.

Persephone's story represents the cyclic nature of life: just like spring comes after winter, our lives go through ups and downs. There is always light after the darkest hour. This myth tells you to keep the faith, even if you are going through winter in your life. Sometimes we make mistakes, just like Persephone when she ate the pomegranate; but there is always a way to bring spring back.

Persephone's symbols

Persephone's symbols are the pomegranate, the deer and the bat, a wreath of flowers and a torch to light the Underworld.

How Persephone can help you

You can work with Persephone's energy for the next eight weeks. You will notice a drawing of a pomegranate under each day's header. This is a reminder to become friends with your past mistakes and to learn to love yourself today, no matter what happened yesterday.

Day 1:

I am my first priority.

From today on, you are going to be your very first priority. Nothing comes first. Think about times when you didn't put your own wellbeing first, and how it ended up. Then reflect about how you can change this pattern from now on.

Gratitude Journal

Today I am thankful for…

Day 2:

I know how to listen to my inner voice.

That's it. Listen. Spend the day listening to what your inner voice has to tell you. Then write down some of your most interesting thoughts.

Gratitude Journal

Today I am thankful for…

Day 3:

The past is gone and my focus is on tomorrow.

Write down the things you want to leave in the past and think about a brighter future. What would life look like without the things which burden you?

Gratitude Journal

Today I am thankful for…

Day 4:

I welcome new adventures.

Imagine the most exciting adventure which could happen to you tomorrow. Write a short story about it. You don't have to keep things realistic: allow yourself to dream big.

_____
_____
_____
_____
_____
_____
_____
_____
_____

Gratitude Journal

Today I am thankful for…

_____
_____
_____
_____

Day 5:

My heart knows the answers.

Our heart knows everything about love and feelings. Is your heart happy? What does your heart want to tell you about your emotional state and your relationships?

_____
_____
_____
_____
_____
_____
_____
_____
_____
_____

Gratitude Journal

Today I am thankful for…

_____
_____
_____
_____

Day 6:

I set boundaries when needed.

Setting boundaries is an extremely important step in your quest for a better you. Is anyone overstepping your boundaries?

_____
_____
_____
_____
_____
_____
_____
_____
_____

Gratitude Journal

Today I am thankful for…

_____
_____
_____
_____

Day 7:

I can deal with it.

You can. Keep this affirmation with you for the whole day. Think about something which overwhelms you and imagine your life when that issue is resolved.

Gratitude Journal

Today I am thankful for…

Day 8:

Every cloud has a silver lining.

There are difficult days. There are times when we feel hopeless. Repeat today's affirmation and believe in it. Write about your very own cloud, and make an effort to find a silver lining in it.

Gratitude Journal

Today I am thankful for…

Day 9:

The Wheel of the Universe is about to turn in my favor.

Was there a time in the past when the *Wheel of Fortune* turned suddenly and your luck changed unexpectedly for the better? Imagine this could happen tomorrow. What would it look like?

Gratitude Journal

Today I am thankful for…

Day 10:

I am not my mistakes.

Your past mistakes don't define you. They are in the past, and you can do better the next time. Write or draw about a mistake you made and then cross it out or erase it until you can't see it anymore. Imagine it disappears as you do it. Say good-bye and remind yourself you know better now. Feel free from that weight. Breathe.

Gratitude Journal

Today I am thankful for…

Day 11:

I have people I trust.

Who are they? If they haven't appeared in your life yet, imagine that person from your future vividly. Imagine the feeling of talking to a true friend. Imagine what they look like, their gestures and how they look at you as you talk to them.

Gratitude Journal

Today I am thankful for…

Day 12:

I know how to start a difficult conversation, and I do it timely.

Is there anything important you should have said to someone, but you never had the courage to do it? Did you ever have to start a difficult conversation in the past? How did it go?

Gratitude Journal

Today I am thankful for...

Day 13:

I am immune to unhealthy temptation.

Temptation takes many shapes. Persephone ate the pomegranate and was forced to stay in the Underworld because of that. What is your pomegranate? Is it procrastination, anger, something else? Imagine a life free from it. You can finish this sentence: *"I am free from … now, and I'm happy and grateful for it."*

Gratitude Journal

Today I am thankful for…

Day 14:

I can do anything I put my mind to.

Today, set a minor goal. It should be something small and useful which requires some effort from your side. For example, challenge yourself to exercise for twenty minutes during the next three days, or skip one cup of coffee or soda for a whole week. Write it down so you don't forget about it. This will help you prove yourself that you can do anything you put your mind to.

Gratitude Journal

Today I am thankful for…

Day 15:

I recognize the right choices.

Reflect about your past choices and how they influenced your present.
"*I am so thankful because now I have clarity to recognize the right choices.*"

Gratitude Journal

Today I am thankful for…

Day 16:

I can help people in need.

Take a couple of minutes to remember those you helped in the past. How did helping them help *you*?

Gratitude Journal

Today I am thankful for…

Day 17:

I know when to move on.

Was there a moment in your life when you realized it was time to move on? Are you still grieving for long-gone things or relationships? Is there anything you must leave behind now in order to blossom?

Gratitude Journal

Today I am thankful for…

Day 18:

I am creative.

We all are creative. Some can bake delicious cakes, while others love to sing, write or draw. You don't have to do anything perfectly: it's enough if you enjoy it. What is your creative gift?

Gratitude Journal

Today I am thankful for…

Day 19:

A new beginning is awaiting.

Think about that new beginning in front of you. What, of all things, do you wish the most?

Gratitude Journal

Today I am thankful for…

Day 20:

I can manage work and family perfectly.

How do you manage your work or study responsibilities, and how does it impact the relationships with those you love? Is there room for improvement? How?

Gratitude Journal

Today I am thankful for…

Day 21:

I stick to good habits.

Some consider 21 the magical number of days to create a habit. Although some people might need more and some people less time[4], you are on your way now that you have been journaling for 21 days on a row. Write a thank-you note to yourself for sticking to this writing habit for three weeks.

_____
_____
_____
_____
_____
_____
_____
_____
_____
_____

Gratitude Journal

Today I am thankful for…

_____
_____
_____
_____

---

[4] *European Journal of Social Psychology,* **https://onlinelibrary.wiley.com/doi/abs/10.1002/ejsp.674**, *How are habits formed: Modelling habit formation in the real world,* *(Online, 2019)*

Day 22:

I believe in myself.

Write down at least one reason why you believe in yourself. What abilities do you possess? What about yourself makes you feel the most confident?

Gratitude Journal

Today I am thankful for…

Day 23:

I cherish my inner child.

Your *inner child* is the childlike part of your personality; the side of you who still feels like a little, helpless, love-seeking child. Some people feel their child side was wounded in the past. Others have no problems at all, and their inner child feels happy and safe. In any case, take time today to write a love message to your inner child. Tell them now they are loved, protected and understood.

Gratitude Journal

Today I am thankful for…

Day 24:

I communicate thoughtfully and clearly.

Clear communication is the basis of good teamwork, and teamwork is necessary to achieve larger projects. Think about the way you communicate with others. Is it ideal? Do you lose your temper easily, or keep silent to avoid conflict? How could you do better?

Gratitude Journal

Today I am thankful for…

Day 25:

I dare to be myself.

Have you ever had to hide or lie because you didn't dare to be yourself? Do you think it was the right choice at that time? Would you do the same today?

Gratitude Journal

Today I am thankful for…

Day 26:

I can love unconditionally.

    Imagine a life where you love without expecting anything back, and you can be happy no matter what others do or don't. True happiness doesn't depend on others, but on yourself. Write about loving things you do (or did in the past) without expecting anything in return. You can start with: ***"I'm proud of myself because…"***

Gratitude Journal

Today I am thankful for…

Day 27:

I know when it's time to wait.

What is your attitude towards waiting and exercising patience? Does waiting make you nervous?

Gratitude Journal

Today I am thankful for…

Day 28:

I am focused.

Your task for today is to focus and get rid of scattered thoughts. What should be your main focus right now? Write it into the circle. What thoughts are secondary and can wait? Write about those in the rectangles.

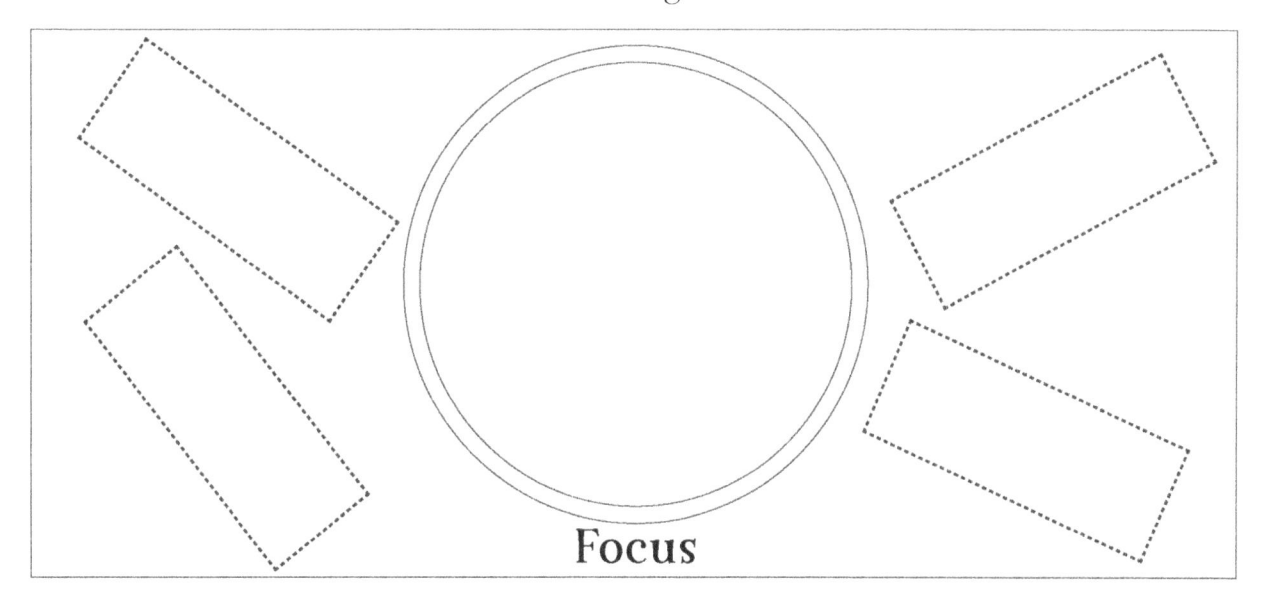

Focus

Gratitude Journal

Today I am thankful for…

_____
_____
_____
_____
_____

Day 29:

My ancestors are proud of me.

"Dear ancestors, you can be proud of me because…"

Gratitude Journal

Today I am thankful for…

Day 30:

I get rid of what I don't need anymore.

Make a list of things you don't need anymore. Would you do better without them?

Gratitude Journal

Today I am thankful for…

Day 31:

Darkness is just a moment before dawn.

Persephone comes back from the Underworld every year, and that's when Demeter allows the spring to start anew. If there are any negative things going on in your life, remind yourself this is just the moment before dawn. ***"I am thankful, because… is about to end, and… awaits me."***

Gratitude Journal

Today I am thankful for…

Day 32:

My good deeds are always rewarded.

Some like to call it *karma*, meaning good actions bring good luck or *what goes around comes around*. Have you ever experienced this phenomenon in real life?

Gratitude Journal

Today I am thankful for…

Day 33:

Heartbreak is meant to free us me from further suffering.

Did you ever feel heartbroken? How did it make you stronger, or kept you from suffering for days on end? Did you learn anything from that experience?

Gratitude Journal

Today I am thankful for…

Day 34:

I always find the best way out.

Sometimes life feels like a complicated labyrinth. But there is always a way out. Think about a situation when you had to find a way out of a problematical issue and you succeeded. ***"I am thankful and proud of myself, because I managed to…"***

Gratitude Journal

Today I am thankful for…

Day 35:

I am a child of Mother Earth, and her healing heals all of us.

Think about ways you could help our Mother Earth heal by reducing your impact. Make a list, which could include for example: joining a cleaning campaign, recycling at home or refusing single-use items.

Gratitude Journal

Today I am thankful for…

Day 36:

I find solutions instead of worrying needlessly.

Think about an issue which worries you. Write and brainstorm for possible solutions. If you are really stuck, think about people you could ask for advice.

Gratitude Journal

Today I am thankful for…

Day 37:

I am loved.

You are loved, because we all are. Out there, someone loves you. Who could it be? It may be your partner, a Higher Presence, your children, your pets, or even someone you don't know yet. Write a few sentences with the following pattern: *"I am thankful because... loves me."*

_____
_____
_____
_____
_____
_____
_____
_____
_____
_____

Gratitude Journal

Today I am thankful for...

_____
_____
_____
_____

Day 38:

I see my dreams materialize in front of me.

Manifestation means *giving physical form to our dreams.* Choose one of your dreams. Describe it. How does it feel to achieve your dream? Where are you? What are you wearing? What is the weather? What can you smell in the air? You can write something like this: **"I am grateful because... is going to happen very soon, and it will look and feel like this: ..."**

Gratitude Journal

Today I am thankful for…

Day 39:

My home is only open to those who deserve it.

What do you do when someone comes uninvited? Think about loving but firm ways to keep unwanted visits away from your personal space.

Gratitude Journal

Today I am thankful for…

Day 40:

I spend my money in smart ways.

What have been your smartest investments so far? Make a list. You can include anything, from a long-lasting used car to a thrifted wedding dress. ***"I am thankful I invested my money in…, because…"***

Gratitude Journal

Today I am thankful for…

Day 41:

There is a Goddess in me.

Write a brief starting with: *"I am aware of the beauty and magic inside of me. They manifest to the world in the following ways..."*

Gratitude Journal

Today I am thankful for…

Day 42:

Money comes easily to me.

How much money would you need to live a comfortable life? Think about an exact amount and write it down. Then visualize your life when you get the money you need. ***"My ideal cash stash is… My life with (X amount of money) looks like this… I am thankful this amount is about to come to my life very soon."***

Gratitude Journal

Today I am thankful for…

Day 43:

I have the right to take a break when I need it.

Do you ever feel guilty for resting or taking breaks? Why is that?

Gratitude Journal

Today I am thankful for…

Day 44:

Hope lives forever in my heart.

Think about a time when you felt the warmth of hope inside your heart, and that hope helped you carry on. ***"I believe in hope, because…"***

Gratitude Journal

Today I am thankful for…

Day 45:

There is someone out there who needs me.

Who needs you the most right now? Is it you? Is it someone else?

Gratitude Journal

Today I am thankful for…

Day 46:

I'm on the right path.

Today, make a map including a few steps necessary to reach a goal of your choice. Briefly describe each step to get from where you are now to where you want to be. Repeat this process as many times as you want, with different objectives.

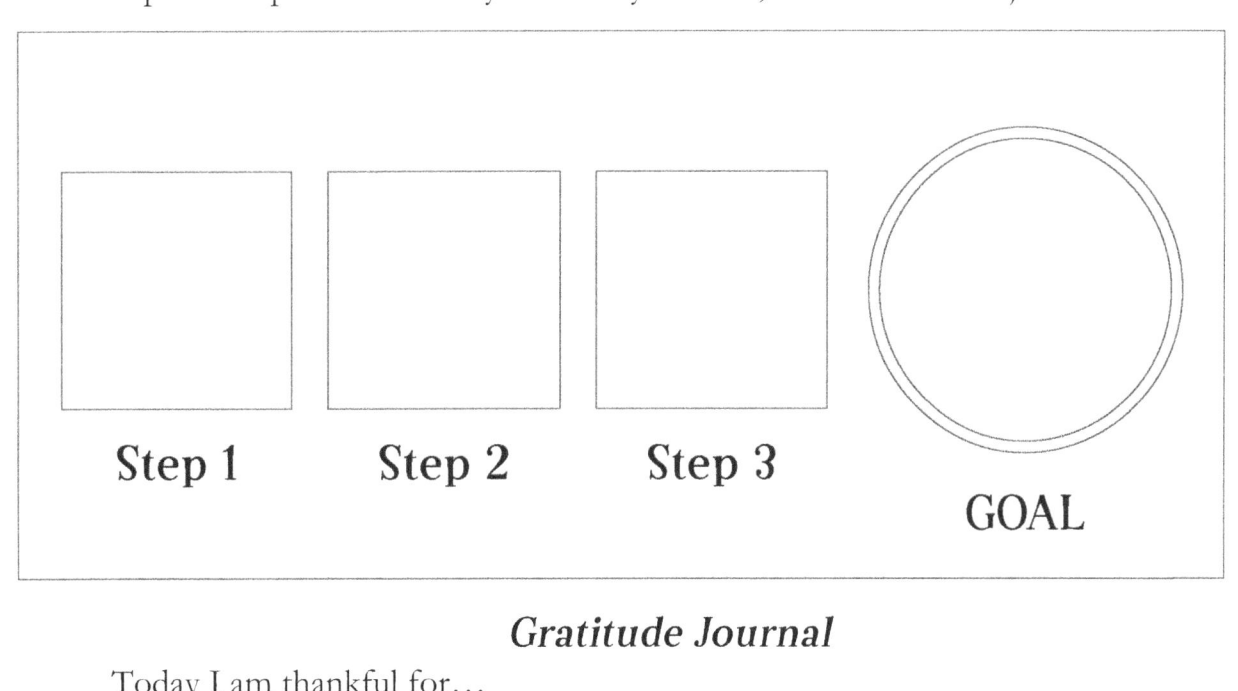

Step 1   Step 2   Step 3   GOAL

Gratitude Journal

Today I am thankful for…

_____
_____
_____
_____
_____

Day 47:

Good opportunities keep coming my way.

Missed opportunities are in the past and shouldn't be dwelled on. It's better to keep your eyes open for new ones, so that you don't miss those, too. *"I am thankful for all the opportunities which are about to come my way, such as..."*

Gratitude Journal

Today I am thankful for...

Day 48:

I fight for fairness.

Do you remember any occasions when you were treated unfairly? Rewrite one of your memories, so that you make the wrong right in your imagination. Give your memory a happy ending where you stand for yourself. *"I remember fondly that day when the teacher wanted to ground me for something I hadn't done, but then I explained her clearly what had really happened..."*

Gratitude Journal

Today I am thankful for...

Day 49:

Taking care of myself comes first.

Write down a list of enjoyable small things you never find time to do. They should be simple things which make you feel better, such as going to the hairdresser's, having coffee with a friend or reading a novel. Which one is the easiest to achieve? Which one would you like to do the most? Can you find time this week for at least two of them?

Gratitude Journal

Today I am thankful for…

Day 50:

Money loves me.

Money loves those who love it. If you hate money, or keep saying money is evil, dirty, or corrupting, how can you expect money to come your way? You are probably scaring it off with such negative thoughts! Today, write a love declaration to money. It may feel silly, but this will give it an opportunity to love you back. ***"Dear Money, I love you because you help me (do this and that), and thanks to you I can afford…"***

Gratitude Journal

Today I am thankful for…

Day 51:

I am good at solving problems.

Are you a good problem-solver? Think about a situation in the past that proves you are. If you can't remember any, make up a story which takes place in a near future. *"**I'm glad I'm so good at solving problems, just like I did when…**"*

Gratitude Journal

Today I am thankful for…

Day 52:

I have no time for liars and troublemakers.

Feel free to throw anyone who deserves it into this imaginary bin. Don't worry, you can erase their names later, or make up a fun pseudonym for them.

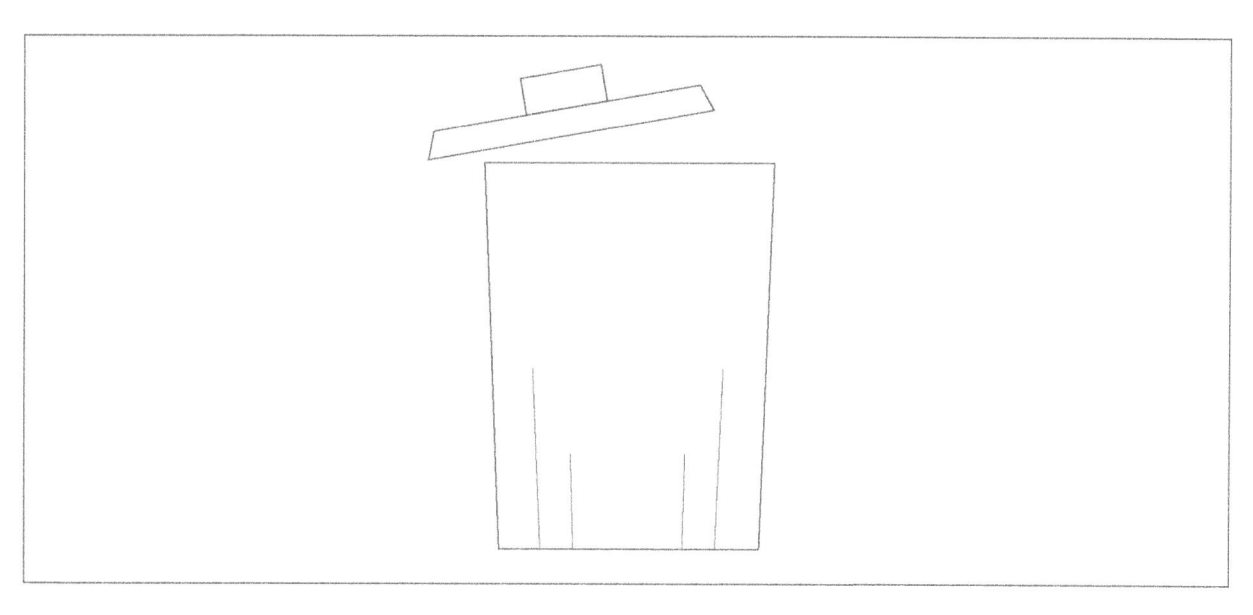

Gratitude Journal

Today I am thankful for…

_____
_____
_____
_____
_____

Day 53:

I live in the now.

Write something on each square. Which of the squares below is easier to write in and read from? The dark square labeled *Past*? Probably not. The gray square labeled *Future*? That one is a bit easier, but still, not as much as the **NOW**. Remind yourself about these squares when you start reliving negative situations from the past or worrying about the future. Stay in the white square!

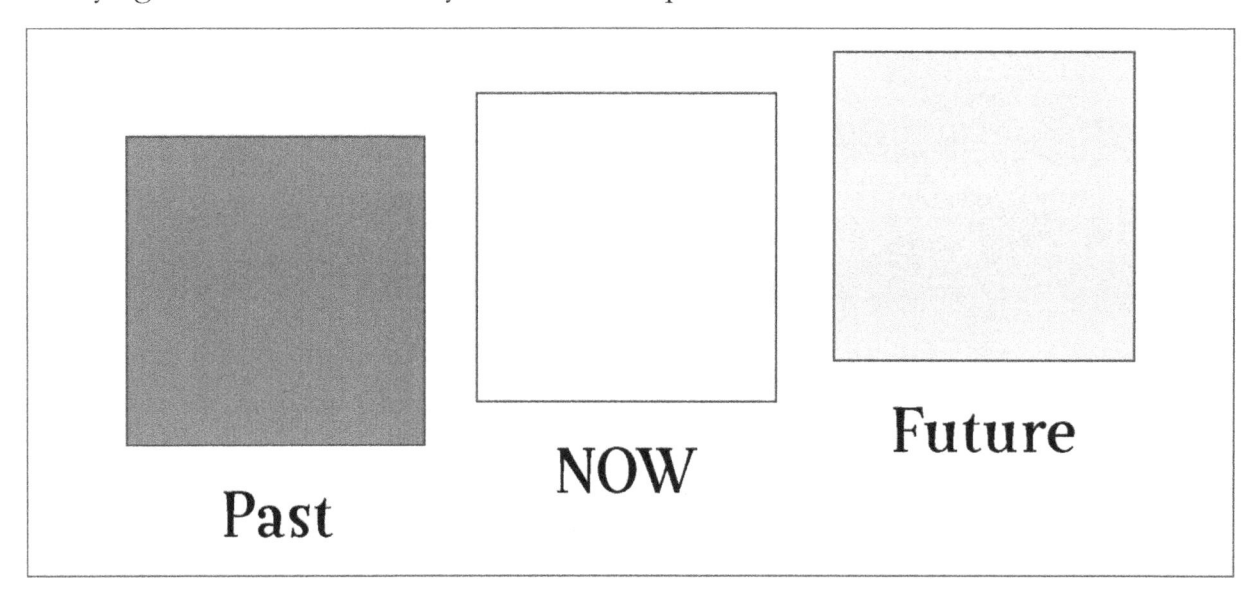

Past **NOW** **Future**

Gratitude Journal

Today I am thankful for…

Day 54:

My loved ones always support me.

There may have been times when you were not supported by those you loved. Think about times when you had/hadn't their support. Imagine having that support unconditionally and give thanks as if you had it already. ***"I'm so thankful for X's and Y's unconditional support when*** *(this and that happened)*/ ***because…"***

Gratitude Journal

Today I am thankful for…

Day 55:

I open my arms to abundance.

There is enough abundance for all of us. The magic recipe starts with believing it, sharing and not being too greedy. Greet *Lady Abundance* and explain her where to find you and why. ***"Dear Lady Abundance…"***

Gratitude Journal
Today I am thankful for…

Day 56:

There is a creative fire inside of me.

What lights your creative fire?

Gratitude Journal

Today I am thankful for…

Day 57:

Sorrow is always temporary.

The cycles of the Universe are ever changing. Sorrow and grief never last forever. Allow yourself to feel sad for the things you lost in the past, and remind yourself that acceptance is on the horizon. Where are you on this ladder right now?

1. I allow myself to be sad when I need it.
2. I accept whatever happened.
3. Life is bright again.

Gratitude Journal

Today I am thankful for…

_____
_____
_____
_____

Day 58:

My talents are blossoming.

Write down one of your many talents and virtues on each petal of the blossoming flower below.

I possess   many talents.

Gratitude Journal

Today I am thankful for…

_____
_____
_____
_____
_____

Day 59:

No burden is too heavy for me.

What is your heaviest burden right now? Find one good thing about it and complete the following sentence: ***"I am grateful for…, because it's teaching me… and I trust I will be able to…"***

_____
_____
_____
_____
_____
_____
_____
_____
_____
_____

Gratitude Journal

Today I am thankful for…

_____
_____
_____
_____

Day 60:

I am a physical and spiritual being.

We all have different beliefs, and that's perfectly okay. Do you believe humans have a spirit? Do you think there is anything beyond your physical body? Does this belief (or lack of it) help you live better?

Gratitude Journal

Today I am thankful for…

Day 61:

I finish what I start.

Unfinished projects take lots of mental energy which could be used to manifest your goals instead. It's like having an appliance on stand-by constantly, using electricity 24/7. Think of the **three** most important **unfinished things** you would like to conclude, and list them below. Even better, write them down on a sticky note and put it in a visible place, to remind you daily you should finish them.

Gratitude Journal

Today I am thankful for…

SECOND JOURNALING CYCLE

Goddess Artemis

Artemis is the Greek Goddess of the hunt, the forests and the moon, and the protector of women and childbirth. You spent the first journaling cycle traveling to the Underworld with Persephone, and now it's time to discover where you are in the cycle of life, find your inner strength and birth the new you. This is a time to sow future happiness and hunt for opportunities.

Artemis's story

Artemis is known as Diana in Roman mythology. She was highly revered in ancient Greece, especially by women. Artemis protects and heals women and young girls: she is known as the guardian of all wild and innocent things. She also aids with childbirth. But despite her protective side, Artemis is to be feared, too: her arrows are fast and unerring, and they can bring sudden, unexpected death.

Artemis is a wild and independent soul. She enjoys roaming the hills and practicing archery with her golden bow and arrows. She is usually accompanied by wild creatures, such as deer and dogs. She vowed never to marry and remain forever a maiden, because she was self-governing and didn't need a man to be complete. In ancient Greece, that was a very brave thing to do for a woman. Many males tried to get Artemis for themselves, some of them forcefully (Hades and Persephone's theme is fairly recurring in Greek mythology), but she always knew how to defend herself with her own weapons (her bow, in this case). Artemis was strong and smart, and very capable of defending herself and doing anything on her own.

Artemis's symbols

Artemis's symbols are the golden bow and arrows; deer, hunting dogs and the moon. Look at these symbols over each day's affirmation to remind you of Artemis's virtues and how to apply them to your own life.

How Artemis can help you

Artemis represents the wild and innocent creature sleeping inside ourselves.

Her strength radiates from her purity. No-one can defeat Artemis's bow, and she is capable of achieving anything on her own. Look upon Artemis to find the strength to be yourself and realize you don't need anyone to be strong and achieve your goals. Artemis didn't wait for *Prince Charming* to come and save her. She rather chose to help herself. Artemis loves helping women and will gladly support the wildness in your heart, as long as your motives are pure.

Day 62:

I am ready to start the journey of my life.

Where do you want to go?

Gratitude Journal

Today I am thankful for…

Day 63:

I am honest.

Being honest to yourself and others can make your life easier, as long as you are respectful. "***From today on, I promise myself to be as honest as possible, and I will start with…***" You can think about things you should stop doing or things you should have told others a long while ago.

Gratitude Journal

Today I am thankful for…

Day 64:

All the strength I need is already inside of me.

Feel your inner strength today. Feel how it shields you from all harms the environment throws at you. Describe or draw your inner strength. What does it feel like? What color and shape is it?

Gratitude Journal

Today I am thankful for…

Day 65:

I am wild.

Was there a time when you were forced to tame the wildness inside your heart? Imagine what it would be like to let your true nature show. Remember Artemis protects all wild things whose intentions are pure: you are safe under her watch. Describe or draw the wild creature living inside of you.

Gratitude Journal

Today I am thankful for…

Day 66:

Inspiration comes my way.

Put your hands in a prayer position, close your eyes and breathe deeply for a few seconds. Ask inspiration to flood you. What do you see in your mind's eye?

Gratitude Journal

Today I am thankful for…

Day 67:

Everyone around me respects me.

Do you feel respected by the people who surround you?

Gratitude Journal

Today I am thankful for…

Day 68:

I leave useless burdens behind.

Artemis is happy with just her bow and arrows: she doesn't need anything else to merrily roam the hills. Make a list and discover what your "*bow and arrows*" are. This might give you an idea of the useless burdens you are carrying in your bag and in your soul.

Gratitude Journal

Today I am thankful for…

Day 69:

I honor everyone's differences.

Do you feel your differences are respected? Do you respect those who are not like you?

Gratitude Journal

Today I am thankful for…

Day 70:

I cherish the innocent child inside of me.

Write about that innocent child who still lives in you. If you have forgotten them, try to imagine what they would look like and what they would love to ask you to do.

Gratitude Journal

Today I am thankful for...

Day 71:

My patience is always rewarded.

What situation in your life requires patience right now? ***"I am sure (this situation) is going to resolve in a positive way, and my patience will be rewarded with…"***

_____
_____
_____
_____
_____
_____
_____
_____
_____
_____

Gratitude Journal

Today I am thankful for…

_____
_____
_____
_____

Day 72:

I have enough material assets.

What material assets would you need for your happiness to be complete? Write a list and thank the Universe for providing you with them in the future.

Gratitude Journal

Today I am thankful for…

Day 73:

Sadness is in the past now.

Whatever made you sad in the past can be left behind. Write down something that tried to suck your happiness and then erase it slowly. Feel how you are erasing it from your mind as you do so.

Gratitude Journal

Today I am thankful for…

Day 74:

My mind is quick and sharp.

Repeat today's affirmation several times during the day. See how answers and solutions start coming faster to your mind. ***"I am thankful for my sharp intellect, which allows me to…"***

Gratitude Journal

Today I am thankful for…

Day 75:

Change is always for the better.

What kind of change do you wish you see in your life? Write it down as it already happened. *"I'm so grateful for... which is about to happen."*

Gratitude Journal

Today I am thankful for...

Day 76:

My ancestors protect me and support me.

Write a brief letter to one or more of your ancestors, and say thanks to them for watching over you.

Gratitude Journal

Today I am thankful for…

Day 77:

I am capable of manifesting my dreams.

Choose one thing you would like to manifest and describe it in all detail: what, when, how, with whom… ***"I am so thankful for… which is about to happen."***

Gratitude Journal

Today I am thankful for…

Day 78:

Mother Earth loves me and all her children.

Think about one think you could do today or tomorrow to give back to Mother Earth and show her your thankfulness. ***"Dear Mother Earth, thank you for your unconditional love. I would like to show you my gratefulness with…"***

Gratitude Journal

Today I am thankful for…

Day 79:

I am loved unconditionally.

"I am worth of being loved unconditionally, and I know there is someone out there who loves and admires me. Thank you, Universe, for connecting me with that person, in the past or in the future."

Gratitude Journal

Today I am thankful for…

Day 80:

I am a good listener.

Make an effort to listen attentively to what others have to say. Write about the most interesting or fun conversation you had lately.

Gratitude Journal

Today I am thankful for…

Day 81:

My arrows are unerring.

Each of us possesses an invisible quiver, full of imaginary golden arrows. Imagine you could pick three arrows from your quiver. The arrows would represent goals, things you need to finish, or people you should talk to or heal your relationship with. Write on each arrow what it represents for you, then send them flying with your magical bow, and be sure they will hit the mark, with Artemis's help.

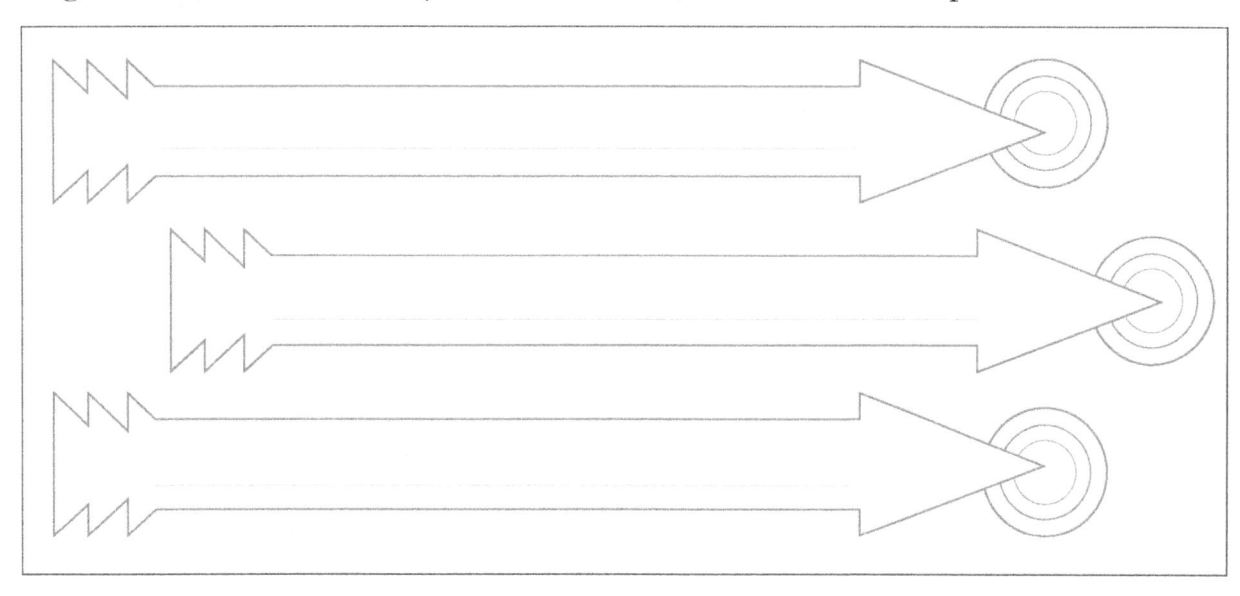

Gratitude Journal

Today I am thankful for…

_____
_____
_____
_____
_____

Day 82:

I always have great ideas.

"I am thankful for all the great ideas I always have, such as…"

Gratitude Journal

Today I am thankful for…

Day 83:

True love is coming my way.

*"I am grateful for true love, which is (making/going to make) **my life better in so many ways:** ... **and I** (expect it to arrive/am thankful it arrived) **like this..."**

Gratitude Journal

Today I am thankful for…

Day 84:

Miracles do happen.

Think of the most incredible miracle you would like to see happen. Describe it as it had already happened, or as if it were about to happen tomorrow.

Gratitude Journal

Today I am thankful for…

Day 85:

My home is my temple.

Every Goddess needs a proper temple. Think of a few things you could do to transform your current home in a sacred space.

Gratitude Journal

Today I am thankful for…

Day 86:

My investments pay off.

Whenever we invest in something we hope to see good returns. You invest your time, your love, your effort, your work and of course your money. Think about an investment you have made (it doesn't have to be financial). Imagine it bringing you awesome returns. Describe what it looks like.

Gratitude Journal

Today I am thankful for…

Day 87:

Good things are about to start.

Sometimes the best things start very small. Sometimes losing a small item allows you to meet someone important for your life. Sometimes you find out about your dream job while sitting gloomily in a crowded waiting room. Think about the small beginning of your great future. What could it look like? Make up a story, unleash your imagination!

Gratitude Journal

Today I am thankful for…

Day 88:

I am ready to receive all the blessings of the Universe.

Write about things you can do to prepare better to receive all the blessings the Universe is about to send your way. For example: clean your home of clutter; stop spending your time doing useless tasks, etc.

Gratitude Journal

Today I am thankful for…

Day 89:

I always hope for the best.

Think about a situation which worries you. Any matter which is not looking very promising right now will do for this exercise. Now imagine this situation resolving in the most positive way you can imagine. What would it look like?

Gratitude Journal

Today I am thankful for…

Day 90:

I forgive and move on.

Is there anyone, from your past or your present, who should be forgiven so that you can move on? Sometimes it feels like some people don't deserve to be forgiven. However, *forgiveness is for you, not for them*, so that you can finally sleep at night and stop thinking about them and the wrong they did to you. **"Today I want to forgive... and thank** *(him/her)* **for the lesson they helped me to learn, which was... I let** *(him/her)* **go and will not allow** *(him/her)* **to suck my energy anymore."**

Gratitude Journal

Today I am thankful for...

Day 91:

The sun always shines after a storm.

Think about the last time this happened in real life. Maybe you had an argument, or lost something, or were completely desperate, but it all ended eventually, and you regained your strength. ***"I am proud of myself because I overcame… and I am thankful for (this learning experience)"***

Gratitude Journal

Today I am thankful for…

Day 92:

I allow my voice to be heard.

Write a message to the world around you. What would you like everyone to know? Maybe it's something about you; maybe it's something they are doing wrong... whatever it is, let your voice be heard today.

Gratitude Journal

Today I am thankful for…

Day 93:

I set boundaries without guilt.

Think about a situation where you should set a boundary. ***"I have enough of…"***

Gratitude Journal

Today I am thankful for…

Day 94:

I laugh often.

They say *laughter is the best medicine*. Why not try to laugh a bit more every day? Try to read fun stories and talk to people who lift your spirits. Write about something which made you laugh lately, even if it's silly. If there is nothing you can remember, then look for a joke or a story you can write about.

Gratitude Journal

Today I am thankful for…

Day 95:

I create beautiful memories every day.

Write about one of the most beautiful memories you have. Try to feel as happy as you felt back then.

Gratitude Journal

Today I am thankful for…

Day 96:

I don't allow other people's problems to suck my energy.

Is anyone out there trying to use you like their *emotional trash bin*? You don't have to be your friend's therapist if you don't want to (we have paid professionals for that!). Learn to recognize situations where you are always giving and self-named *friends* are always taking from you. Then brainstorm for ways to reduce this kind of situations.

Gratitude Journal

Today I am thankful for…

Day 97:

I dare to show my true self to the world.

You are unique and you deserve to be seen and heard. Think about one small step you could take in the future to share a glimpse your true self to the wide world.

Gratitude Journal

Today I am thankful for…

Day 98:

I take fair decisions.

When in the past were you (or weren't you) fair to others? How can you be fairer from now on?

_____
_____
_____
_____
_____
_____
_____
_____
_____

Gratitude Journal

Today I am thankful for…

_____
_____
_____
_____

Day 99:

I have the job of my dreams.

What would you like to do every day? It doesn't have to be a paying job. You might want to be a full-time mother, or you may be retired and want to spend your days gardening around your beautiful house. Whatever it is, describe it under these lines with as much detail as possible. You can even make a schedule: *"from 9:00 am to 10:00, I'd like to…"*

Gratitude Journal

Today I am thankful for…

Day 100:

I am good at journaling.

Congratulations! You just wrote in your journal for **one hundred days** on a row. This is yet another proof that ***you can make things happen***. Give yourself a reward and do some freestyle journaling.

Gratitude Journal

Today I am thankful for…

Day 101:

I live in abundance.

Abundance means "*a large amount of something*". What kind of abundance do you have in mind? What is this *something* you need more of in your life?

Gratitude Journal

Today I am thankful for…

Day 102:

I solve conflicts peacefully and without arguments.

Think about the last time you had to solve a conflict. Did you react in the best possible way? What would you have done differently, if you had had more time to think?

Gratitude Journal

Today I am thankful for…

Day 103:

I am a roaring lioness.

Write two things that make you strong. Then roar loudly until it makes you laugh, if you feel like.

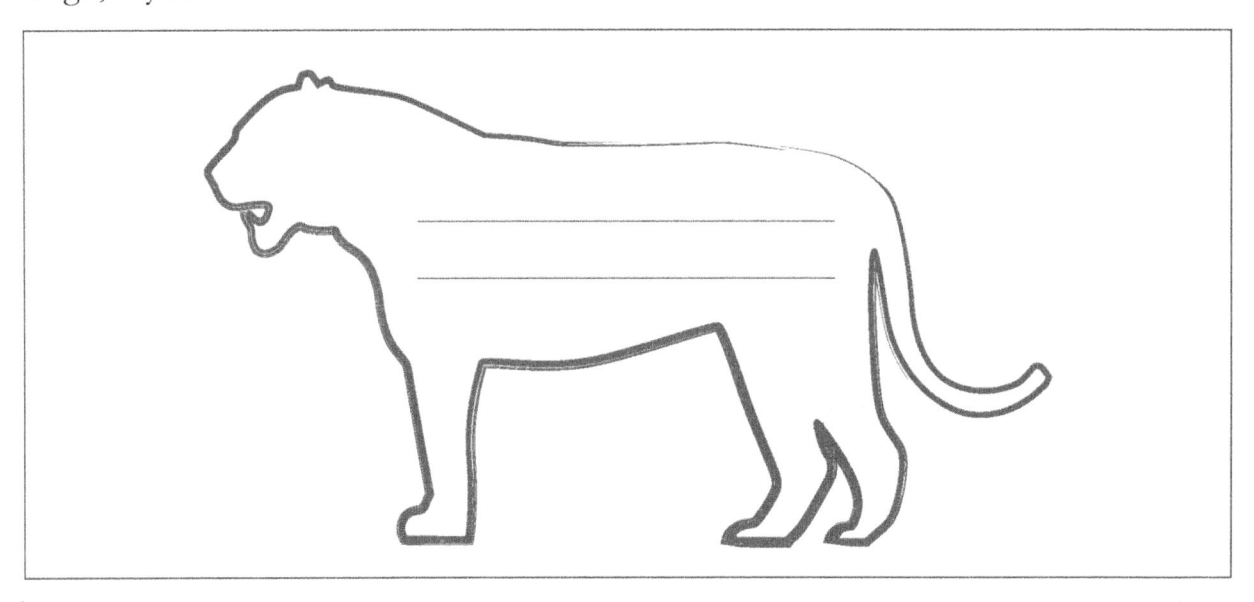

Gratitude Journal

Today I am thankful for…

Day 104:

I fight for my rights.

Do you feel all your rights are being respected? What should you be fighting for right now?

Gratitude Journal

Today I am thankful for…

Day 105:

A new financial opportunity is around the corner.

Imagine you were just offered a really good opportunity related to money. What would it be, how would it happen

Gratitude Journal

Today I am thankful for...

Day 106:

I am excited about the future.

If you often feel apathetic, you are probably missing many opportunities, which are going to knock on someone else's door. People who feel excited about the future seem to have better chances to manifest the future they dream of. Today, make an effort and write about the future, and how excited you feel about every new day. ***"I am so excited about the future, because I trust things are getting better and better with each day that passes…"***

Gratitude Journal

Today I am thankful for…

Day 107:

I always find an easy exit.

Is there a situation in your life you should get out from? Close your eyes and ask the Universe to show you the easiest exit. Write down the answers.

Gratitude Journal

Today I am thankful for…

Day 108:

I have a beautiful family.

Families can differ widely. Your family may be composed of three German shepherds and five cats, or you may have seven loving siblings. Anyhow, we all need to find our tribe. Who is your family?

Gratitude Journal

Today I am thankful for…

Day 109:

Kindness is always returned to the giver.

How can you be kind to others? How have others been kind to you in the past? Is there anything or anyone you could be thankful for?

Gratitude Journal

Today I am thankful for…

Day 110:

I am free from suffering.

Whether you are actually free from suffering or not at the moment, fill in the affirmation: ***"I am thankful because all the suffering caused by… has finally vanished into thin air and has made room for my present life, which I enjoy fully."***

Gratitude Journal

Today I am thankful for…

Day 111:

Writing helps me find my path.

It is said that 111 is a powerful manifestation number. Have you been seeing lots of 11:11 lately? Maybe 22:22? Pay attention for repeating numbers when you check the time, register plates and the like. These are sometimes called *"angel numbers"* and might be a sign of your manifestation energy starting to stir.

It's quite remarkable that you have been writing a journal for 111 days already. How did journaling make your life different up to now?

Gratitude Journal

Today I am thankful for…

Day 112:

I hunt my fears with my golden arrows.

What are the things that keep you awake at night? Imagine they are fluffy black dots flying in the sky. Close your eyes and shoot your golden arrows towards the black dots. See them vanish into thin air. Feel lighter now. Write how you feel afterwards.

Gratitude Journal

Today I am thankful for…

Day 113:

My words are clear and to the point.

Clear communication is a must if you want to reach your goals. Make it a priority to talk clearly and avoid beating about the bush. Think about people you know who are a good example of speaking clearly and to the point.

Gratitude Journal

Today I am thankful for…

Day 114:

Life never presents me with any problems I can't solve.

Write down two or three problems which bother you right now, and brainstorm for solutions.

Gratitude Journal

Today I am thankful for…

Day 115:

I am visible.

Being *in*visible may be comfortable, but it is rarely the best choice. What part of you or your creations is awaiting to be presented to the world? Have you been hiding yourself, or part of yourself?

Gratitude Journal

Today I am thankful for…

Day 116:

I recognize cheaters and cut ties with them timely.

Think about people who abused your trust. Have you talked to them about it and solved the issue, or will you have to cut ties with them eventually?

WHO	WHAT	SOLVED?
		☐
		☐
		☐

Gratitude Journal

Today I am thankful for…

_____
_____
_____
_____

Day 117:

I have good friends.

Who are your true friends? If you feel you have none, describe your ideal friends and thank the Universe for introducing you very soon. ***"I am thankful for the friends (I have/I'm about to meet), because they are.../they will..."***

Gratitude Journal

Today I am thankful for…

Day 118:

I open my heart to the goodness of the Universe.

Imagine the Universe were a big magic fountain springing from the sky. Close your eyes and walk under the gushing water. As your hair and clothes become soaked, imagine your heart as a small crystal box. See the lid of that box opening and becoming full of magic water. What will you use the magic from your crystal box for?

Gratitude Journal

Today I am thankful for…

Day 119:

My hope is everlasting.

There are many stories of famous people who were rejected repeatedly but succeeded in the end. They were often told that they weren't good enough for the job they applied to. Although most stories you will find online are about writers, actors, singers and sportspeople, it works just the same for office clerks, teachers and people going through IVF, to cite a few examples. If you don't know any, try to find some inspirational stories about keeping the faith and journal about one of them.

Gratitude Journal

Today I am thankful for…

Day 120:

My mistakes make me wiser.

Write about a mistake you made and what you learned from it.

Gratitude Journal

Today I am thankful for…

Day 121:

Money is my good friend.

Now that you are good friends with money, invite it for a date and do something together. What would you do? Maybe to shopping? Go to a spa?

Gratitude Journal

Today I am thankful for…

Day 122:

All cycles come to an end.

We humans, and especially women, are cyclical creatures. Our cycles are very much under the influence of the moon. This evening try to look at the moon. If you can't, just imagine it or look at its picture. As you stand under the moon, imagine the power of the moon imbues you with new and clean energy to start a new cycle of your life. *"I'm so happy about this new cycle of my life, in which… will happen."*

Gratitude Journal

Today I am thankful for…

THIRD JOURNALING CYCLE

Goddess Athena

Athena is the Greek Goddess of war and wisdom. Like Artemis, she is a virgin Goddess, and like all virgin Goddesses she is very independent and capable. She was born from the head of Zeus, from which she sprang already as an adult and dressed in full armor. She is a very strong and beloved Goddess and a protector of civilized life. It is said that she provided people on Earth with the knowledge they needed to live in harmony and to win necessary battles. Despite being the Goddess of war, she is also the Goddess of wisdom, and she prefers using her intellect instead of battling when possible. But just like most Greek Goddesses, she can also be ruthless when angry, so her wrath is to be feared.

Goddess Athena can teach us to be brave, but with thoughtfulness. In order to achieve our goals we need clarity and vision. Athena's symbolic animal is the owl, a big-eyed bird of prey who observes all creatures from an elevated position in the sky before attacking.

Athena's story

It is said that Athena's father, Zeus, was afraid of having a child with his wife Metis, Goddess of wisdom, because he knew that such a child would be stronger and smarter than him and might overrule him. So he solved the problem in a very *Olympian* way and gulped his wife whole. It didn't help, though, and he got a terrible headache afterwards as Athena, who had been already conceived, started to grow in his head. His headache was finally relieved when his daughter, Athena, sprung out of his head, fully grown and wearing a golden armor and a spear. She was extremely intelligent indeed, but she didn't steal his throne and ended up becoming his favorite child.

Later, Athena competed with Poseidon in order to see who would become the patron of the city of Athens. In order to decide who was the best fit, they both made an offering to the city. Poseidon offered a spring of sea water, but it wasn't possible to drink from it, so it was useless. Athena then offered the Greek people an olive tree, which would provide food, oil and wood, and was also a symbol of peace. After that, she was declared the winner of the contest and she became the patron and protector of Athens. The city took her name, and the Parthenon was built in her honor.

Athena's symbols

Athena's symbol is the owl, which is also related to wisdom. Other symbols of Athena are the helmet, the spear and the olive tree.

How Athena can help you

Athena's energy is wonderful for journaling. She is wise and thoughtful. She is a warrior, but she relies on strategy. Work with Athena's energy for the next two months and make clarity and wisdom your priority during this period. We need to fight for what we dream of, but it is necessary to have a plan first.

Day 123:

I acquire new wisdom every day.

We all wish to achieve the life of our dreams. But good things take planning and learning. What do you need to learn in order to earn enough money to be satisfied? Do you need to read books? Do you need to finish your degree? Should you have an internship somewhere, or find experts in the subject?

Gratitude Journal

Today I am thankful for…

Day 124:

I believe in new beginnings.

Finish this sentence with a positive statement: ***"today is the first day of…"***

Gratitude Journal

Today I am thankful for…

Day 125:

Bad things are in the past.

Finish this sentence with a positive statement: ***"bad things are in the past, and the future…"***

Gratitude Journal

Today I am thankful for…

Day 126:

I sever all toxic ties.

Are there any toxic ties you should remove from your life? Is it time to borrow Zeus's bolt to break those energy-sucking connections?

Gratitude Journal

Today I am thankful for…

Day 127:

I shine with my inner light.

Close your eyes and imagine a strong light coming from the center of your heart. This is your inner power, shining its magical light on the world. What color is it? Is it cool, or warm? Does it have a shape?

Gratitude Journal

Today I am thankful for…

Day 128:

I never give up.

Think about projects you started but never finished. Maybe it was a painting, or a story, or you promised someone to have coffee together but never called them back. Write down at least one and promise yourself to finish it in the next two weeks.

PROJECT	SCHEDULE	FINISHED?
		☐
		☐
		☐

Gratitude Journal

Today I am thankful for…

Day 129:

I show my true self to the world.

Do you dress in clothes you love? Do you wear your hair the way you want to? Do you say the things you want to say? Are you showing your true self to the world, or are you still hiding in the shadows?

Gratitude Journal

Today I am thankful for…

Day 130:

My falls make me stronger.

Write about an anecdote which proves how strong you can be when you have to.

Gratitude Journal

Today I am thankful for…

Day 131:

My differences are accepted and honored by the community.

What makes you unique? What makes you different from the rest?

Gratitude Journal

Today I am thankful for...

Day 132:

I learn something new every day.

Did you learn anything new today? What was it? It can be something really small. If you didn't, pick a book or open your internet browser and try to learn something you didn't know yet. It can be a recipe, a new word in your language or a foreign one, anything. Make an effort to learn something new every single day: it will keep you young and growing.

Gratitude Journal

Today I am thankful for…

Day 133:

I am spiritual and wise.

Complete this sentence: *"my spiritual side has taught me..."*

Gratitude Journal

Today I am thankful for...

Day 134:

I am strict when it's necessary.

Think about times you had to be strict and that helped you achieve your goals. If you have never been strict enough, think about ways to change this.

Gratitude Journal

Today I am thankful for…

Day 135:

I can teach something to the world.

What can you do better than others? What could you teach those around you? Think about at least one thing you can do better than most people you know.

Gratitude Journal

Today I am thankful for…

Day 136:

Not everyone is worth my time and energy.

Are you wasting your time or energy on someone who doesn't deserve it?

Gratitude Journal

Today I am thankful for…

Day 137:

My heart knows what is best, and I listen to it.

Close your eyes and put your hands over your heart. Feel how it beats and keeps you alive, whether you are asleep or awake. Say thank you to your heart for its work and perseverance. Then ask your heart if it has a positive message for you today. Remain silent and wait to hear words or see images in your head. Write down what you found out, even if today it doesn't make any sense yet. If you get negative words it's probably your fears speaking, so keep trying until you hear something positive.

Gratitude Journal

Today I am thankful for…

Day 138:

I stand up for my beliefs.

What do you believe in? Were your beliefs questioned by others in the past? Did others ever make fun of you for believing in something or someone they considered silly? What did you do about that? How would you react if this happened today?

Gratitude Journal

Today I am thankful for…

Day 139:

I can concentrate.

A scattered mind is not conductive to success. Think about one thing, only one important thing, you should concentrate on these days. What is it?

Gratitude Journal

Today I am thankful for…

Day 140:

I take good care of others.

Have you ever taken care of someone else? It could be your grandparents, your children or your pets. Did it make you feel good, even if they showed no visible thankfulness?

Gratitude Journal

Today I am thankful for…

Day 141:

I travel to wonderful places.

Imagine you were a bird and you could fly anywhere you wanted to. Where would you go right now?

Gratitude Journal

Today I am thankful for…

Day 142:

I trust the process.

Finish this sentence with a positive statement: ***"I trust the process, because…"***

Gratitude Journal

Today I am thankful for…

Day 143:

I am fair.

Think about something you did in the past which proves you are a fair judge and your decisions are impartial. This could be a situation which you could have used for your own benefit, but you didn't. ***"I am proud of myself, because…"***

Gratitude Journal

Today I am thankful for…

Day 144:

I have a superpower.

If you were a Goddess —and who knows, you might be one—, how would people call you? What would your *superpower* be? **"My name is Jane, Goddess of…"**

Gratitude Journal

Today I am thankful for…

Day 145:

I am useful to my community.

Are you useful to your community? Do you help in any way? Are there ways you could collaborate with those around you?

Gratitude Journal

Today I am thankful for…

Day 146:

I am successful at life.

Repeat today's affirmation, then define what *success* means for you. ***"Success is…"***

Gratitude Journal

Today I am thankful for…

Day 147:

Occasional solitude heals my soul.

When was the last time you spent some quiet time with yourself? How do you feel when you are alone?

Gratitude Journal

Today I am thankful for...

Day 148:

I am open to the messages of my intuition.

For the next days, pay close attention to small signs and messages. Look at leafs, birds, random written words you see on the street, etc. Remember most negative thoughts arise from fear and not from intuition itself. Focus on the positive and finish this sentence: *"my intuition wants me to know…"*

Gratitude Journal

Today I am thankful for…

Day 149:

I am a protector.

Athena protected the city of Athens. And you? Who might need your protection, and how?

Gratitude Journal

Today I am thankful for…

Day 150:

My perseverance is always rewarded.

150 days of journaling. What will you choose as a reward for your perseverance?

Gratitude Journal

Today I am thankful for…

Day 151:

I am merciful.

A good Goddess of war knows when it's time to show her mercy. Think about those who insulted you or treated you badly in the past. Maybe it happened in high school, or at a former job or relationship. How can you be better than them? How could you show your mercy if you met them again?

Gratitude Journal

Today I am thankful for…

Day 152:

The world loves me for what I am.

Write down one of the hundreds of reasons why you deserve to be loved.

Gratitude Journal

Today I am thankful for…

Day 153:

Others listen to my wise words.

Who listens to you? Who asks you for advice?

Gratitude Journal

Today I am thankful for…

Day 154:

I am empathic, but I don't allow others to use me.

It's good to listen to others and help them with their problems. But it's not okay to allow energy vampires to suck your life energy. Are there any energy vampires around you?

Gratitude Journal

Today I am thankful for…

Day 155:

I find creative ways to solve problems.

Write down three wishes, no matter how difficult or absurd. Now imagine you met a genie, and he promised to grant you *only one wish*. Find a creative way to get all your three wishes at once!

Gratitude Journal

Today I am thankful for…

Day 156:

I am capable of taking care of my own life.

Is there anything you need to solve in order to be more independent or take better care of yourself? Maybe pass an exam? Get your driving license? Find your own place to live? What is it?

Gratitude Journal

Today I am thankful for…

Day 157:

I have the courage to express my true feelings.

Have you been hiding any feelings inside you, good or bad?

Gratitude Journal

Today I am thankful for…

Day 158:

I have good teachers.

Write a thank you message to the best teachers you had in your life.

Gratitude Journal

Today I am thankful for…

Day 159:

I work on discovering my life purpose daily.

Write about ways you can discover your life purpose. *Hint: journaling is one of them.*

Gratitude Journal

Today I am thankful for…

Day 160:

My body and mind work perfectly.

Describe how perfectly your body and mind work. You can also make a drawing instead. Only write or draw good things. ***"I am thankful for…"***

Gratitude Journal

Today I am thankful for…

Day 161:

I am unique.

Write at least one thing which makes you unique.

Gratitude Journal

Today I am thankful for…

Day 162:

My mind is sharp.

How do you keep your mind sharp? Write at least one way you can feed your problem solving skills. It can be a hobby, such as reading, doing crossword or Sudoku puzzles.

Gratitude Journal

Today I am thankful for…

Day 163:

I am strong enough.

How does it feel to be strong enough? What would you do if you had infinite strength?

Gratitude Journal

Today I am thankful for…

Day 164:

I have enough love for everyone who needs me.

Draw a big circle and start writing the name of all the people you love inside of it. If you run out of space, that's a good sign.

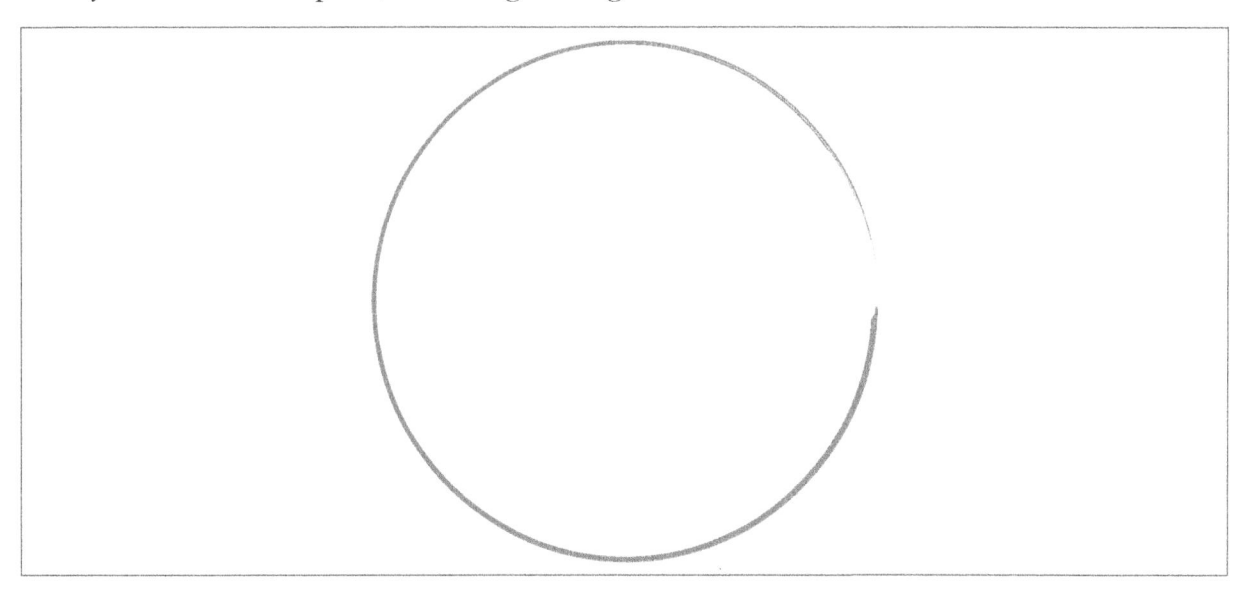

Gratitude Journal

Today I am thankful for…

_____
_____
_____
_____
_____

Day 165:

I am thankful and I see the glass half full.

Think about a situation which has been worrying you lately. Now try to see the glass half full. Find one good thing in that situation, or imagine the best outcome possible becoming true.

Gratitude Journal

Today I am thankful for…

Day 166:

I am wealthy.

When would you consider yourself wealthy? ***"When I have/achieve ……. I will consider myself wealthy"***.

Gratitude Journal

Today I am thankful for…

Day 167:

I have wise counsellors.

Who is your *wise counsellor*? If you have none, imagine what this person would be like and what they could teach you about. What would you ask your wise counsellors about?

Gratitude Journal

Today I am thankful for…

Day 168:

Abundance is a fountain and I drink from it.

Close your eyes and imagine the fountain of abundance in front of you. Cup your hands and drink as much as you need, until you are not thirsty anymore. What would you do if you had all the abundance in the world?

Gratitude Journal

Today I am thankful for…

Day 169:

Every day I am one step closer to my dream home.

If you already live in your dream home, use today's journaling to give thanks. If not, write about your dream home.

Gratitude Journal

Today I am thankful for…

Day 170:

I deserve time for myself.

How do you feel when you tell your friends or family that you need time for yourself? When are you going to take yourself out on a date?

Gratitude Journal

Today I am thankful for…

Day 171:

I say goodbye when necessary.

Write down one thing you should get rid of in your life. Then say goodbye to it. ***"Today I want to say goodbye to... and thank it for..."***

Gratitude Journal

Today I am thankful for...

Day 172:

I visualize my goals every day.

Make a small list of short-term goals. After you write down each of them, try to visualize it as it had already happened.

Gratitude Journal

Today I am thankful for…

Day 173:

I deserve a respectful partner.

If you already have a respectful partner, take some time today to be thankful about it. If you don't, imagine a conversation with your ideal partner. How would you both react when discussing something you don't agree about?

Gratitude Journal

Today I am thankful for…

Day 174:

I deserve prosperity.

What will be the first three things you will buy once you achieve the prosperity you dream about?

1.

2.

3.

Gratitude Journal

Today I am thankful for…

Day 175:

I have everything I need.

Manifesting new things and situations is awesome. But take some time today to list all the good things you already have in your life. If you need extra space (hopefully you will!), use the blank pages at the end for this exercise.

Gratitude Journal

Today I am thankful for…

Day 176:

I am looking forward to a new, better chapter of my life.

Imagine you could start a new chapter of your life tomorrow. Describe your ideal day from morning to night. What would you do? Who would you meet, and where?

Gratitude Journal

Today I am thankful for…

Day 177:

I work hard to achieve my goals.

They say "*God helps those who help themselves*". How are you working actively to become better? Are you working out, eating healthy, educating yourself…? If you aren't (yet), what is something helpful you could add to your daily routine?

Gratitude Journal

Today I am thankful for…

Day 178:

I know who to trust.

Who are the people you trust the most? Write about them today, and thank them for being always by your side.

Gratitude Journal

Today I am thankful for…

Day 179:

I am pure of heart and body.

People who are pure of heart wish well to everyone around them. Choose three people you know and make a good wish in their behalf.

1.

2.

3.

Gratitude Journal

Today I am thankful for…

Day 180:

I am a being of light.

Imagine you were an angel. You might actually be an earthly angel, if you believe in such things. Who would you shed your light on today?

Gratitude Journal

Today I am thankful for…

Day 181:

I know how to have fun.

Write about something enjoyable you did lately.

Gratitude Journal

Today I am thankful for…

Day 182:

I am generous.

Write about something generous you did lately.

Gratitude Journal

Today I am thankful for…

Day 183:

There is always someone ready to support me.

Today, write about your support network and what you do to give back to them. ***"I am thankful for... and I want to show them my gratefulness in this way..."***

Gratitude Journal

Today I am thankful for...

Day 184:

My dreams are coming true.

"Today I am thankful for... which is about to happen."

Gratitude Journal

Today I am thankful for…

FOURTH JOURNALING CYCLE

Goddess Aphrodite

Aphrodite is the Greek Goddess of beauty and love (both physical and platonic love). For the next two months, focus yourself on the love you have and the love you want. Remember that true love starts by loving yourself and your body deeply, so that you can later extend it outwards and share it with others.

Aphrodite's story

Some myths say Aphrodite was born from the foam of the sea. She rose from the waves fully grown, nude and perfectly beautiful. She was loved by many and had plenty of romances with Gods and mortals, even after marrying Hephaestus. She never had enough partners, but she rarely opened her heart to anyone. Her body was the epitome of beauty and perfection, and she was a symbol of passion, fertility, procreation, pleasure and desire.

Aphrodite's symbols

Aphrodite's symbols are seashells and other marine creatures (because she was born from the sea), and also roses and doves, which are connected to love and beauty.

How Aphrodite can help you

Aphrodite was attractive and was also very much aware and proud of her own beauty. Unlike her, many people are beautiful but fail to see their own magnificence. We must learn to love ourselves and our bodies, because it's impossible to find love outside if you don't love yourself first. Aphrodite teaches us that love must radiate from our core, and that pleasure should not come hand in hand with guilt. For the next two months, use Aphrodite's archetype to remind yourself daily that you are beautiful, and worthy of the highest forms of love and respect.

Day 185:

I am loving and loved.

"I am so thankful for all the love I give and receive daily…"

Gratitude Journal

Today I am thankful for…

Day 186:

I love every inch of my body.

Write about the favorite parts of your body, like this: ***"dear hands, I love you because you help me to write, caress and touch…"***

Gratitude Journal

Today I am thankful for…

Day 187:

Every inch of my physical body is sacred.

List your least favorite parts or traits of your body. Then go through the list and tell to each of them that you love them. For example: *"dear nose, I love you because you help me to breathe,"* or: *"dear scar, I love you because you remind me that I survived that accident."* If you can't find anything good to write about them, just say *"Dear X, I love you."*

Gratitude Journal

Today I am thankful for…

Day 188:

My body is my temple.

Make a list of the things you ate today. Are you mindful of what you put into your body? If you aren't, today is a good day to start. You can start a food diary or join a healthy eating group if you think you might need help with this.

Gratitude Journal

Today I am thankful for…

Day 189:

I am beautiful.

Finish this sentence: ***"I am beautiful because…"*** Remember to address your inner and outer beauty.

Gratitude Journal

Today I am thankful for…

Day 190:

I break bad habits and start healthy ones.

What are your bad habits? What triggers them?

Gratitude Journal

Today I am thankful for…

Day 191:

The future is bright.

List three reasons why your future is bright. Use your imagination.

Gratitude Journal

Today I am thankful for…

Day 192:

I only gift my time to honest people.

Loving yourself includes respecting yourself and making yourself respected. Who have you been gifting your free time lately? Did they deserve the gift of your time?

Gratitude Journal

Today I am thankful for…

Day 193:

I deserve pleasure in my life.

What things give you pleasure? Think about all kinds of things, even the small ones count. Some examples might be a cup of coffee in the mornings or standing under a warm shower.

Gratitude Journal

Today I am thankful for…

Day 194:

I am meant to succeed.

Write about small victories you have experienced in the past.

Gratitude Journal

Today I am thankful for…

Day 195:

There is always someone ready to support me.

Write about your support network (real or ideal).

Gratitude Journal

Today I am thankful for…

Day 196:

I am blossoming.

How are you blossoming? How have you changed for the better lately?

Gratitude Journal

Today I am thankful for…

Day 197:

My thoughts contain valuable information.

Make a conscious effort to avoid ruminating thoughts during your day to day: avoid thinking fruitlessly about the same issue on and on. Take a few deep breaths and try to clear your mind. Let new thoughts appear. What ideas come to mind first?

Gratitude Journal

Today I am thankful for…

Day 198:

I take care of my physical body.

If you don't have one yet, make a plan to take better care of your physical body. You might include a face cleansing routine in the evenings, finding some yoga videos online or committing to running for fifteen minutes every morning or evening.

Gratitude Journal

Today I am thankful for…

Day 199:

True love is my birthright.

You were born to love and to be loved. Have you ever experienced true love? If you haven't yet, how do you imagine it? ***"I am thankful for true love, which in my life manifests like this…"***

Gratitude Journal

Today I am thankful for…

Day 200:

I am patient.

Patience is an incredibly useful virtue. You can manifest anything, but sometimes it takes time. Today, make a small list of goals and decide by when you should be able to accomplish them. Example: *"get a new car: in six months"*. Don't forget about your reward for these 200 days of journaling.

Gratitude Journal

Today I am thankful for…

Day 201:

My home is a sacred place.

Your home is like the outer layer of your body. How can you make your home a sacred place? What can you do to bring your current home a step closer to the home of your dreams?

Gratitude Journal

Today I am thankful for…

Day 202:

I always invest my time in worthy tasks.

What do you do when you have some free time in your hands? Do you browse social networks or watch videos mindlessly? Or do you invest this time in things which will help you become who you want to be? Make a list of things you could do with those ten minute breaks we all have a few times per day. For example: read an eBook, do some yoga, meditate, call someone, etc…

Gratitude Journal

Today I am thankful for…

Day 203:

I recognize the truth.

"I am thankful to the Universe, because I am about to learn the truth about…"

Gratitude Journal

Today I am thankful for…

Day 204:

The cycles of life will put everyone in their place eventually.

Think about a time when this affirmation became true. If you can't remember any examples, use your imagination to make up a story about the future.

Gratitude Journal

Today I am thankful for…

Day 205:

The Universe protects me.

Trust the Universe to protect those whose intentions are pure. Draw yourself in the space below. Then, draw a circle around you. Imagine there is a protective bubble around you. Color it and decorate it. Whenever you feel the need, imagine that protective bubble around you, with all its colors.

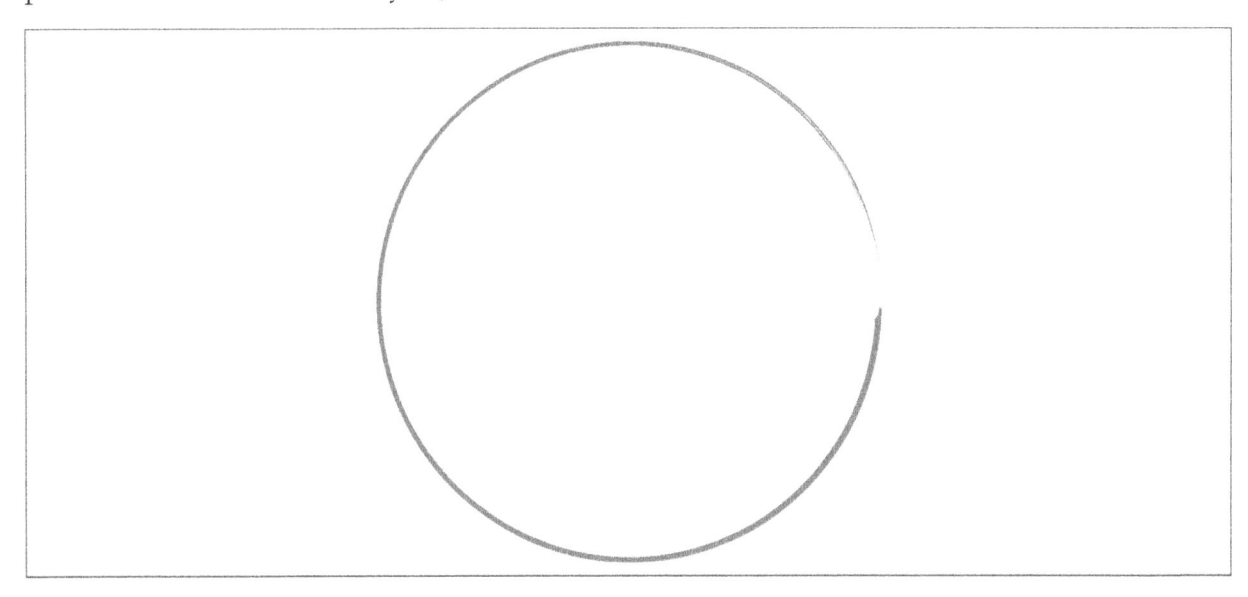

Gratitude Journal

Today I am thankful for…

Day 206:

I am moderate in my actions and my decisions.

Think about ways you can practice moderation in your life (you can apply moderation to eating, drinking, working or any aspect of your life where it might be necessary).

Gratitude Journal
Today I am thankful for…

Day 207:

I know how to turn my back to things which harm me.

Think about things which cause you harm and ways to turn your back to them.

Gratitude Journal

Today I am thankful for…

Day 208:

I shape the path towards my goals every day.

Write down two of your current goals. What is the first step to achieve each of them?

	GOAL	FIRST STEP
1		
2		

Gratitude Journal

Today I am thankful for…

_____
_____
_____
_____

Day 209:

I deserve to be listened to.

Who listens to you and remembers what you say? And who seems to forget everything you tell them?

Gratitude Journal

Today I am thankful for…

Day 210:

I have good ideas.

Do some automatic writing. Just start to write without paying attention to the words. Let the pen run free. Depending on your style, you might need more space, in this case continue in the pages at the end of the book or take a new sheet of paper for this exercise. You can start with this: *"today I had an idea…"*

Gratitude Journal

Today I am thankful for…

Day 211:

I have met the love of my dreams.

Describe how you will meet the love of your dreams. Where? When? What are you wearing? If you know them already, describe how you actually met.

Gratitude Journal

Today I am thankful for…

Day 212:

I pay attention to the hidden messages in my dreams.

Try to remember a good dream you had, and describe it. If you never remember your dreams, you can write what you would like to dream, and maybe you will actually dream about it tonight.

Gratitude Journal

Today I am thankful for…

Day 213:

I am a hard worker.

Write about the best side of your current work (or lack of it). Find reasons why this job helps you grow as a person.

Gratitude Journal
Today I am thankful for…

Day 214:

I have no fear.

Fear is a paralyzing monster. Those who suffer it daily know it's true. Sometimes fears are founded, such as those triggered by close dangers (f. e., war, poverty, aggressive people, etc.). Other times, fear is just fed by our own minds. Today, spend the day trying to starve your unfounded fears. Is there anything you are afraid of which is very unlikely to happen? Write it down and then rationalize why you shouldn't be afraid of it.

Gratitude Journal

Today I am thankful for…

Day 215:

I am becoming the best version of myself.

Describe the best future version of yourself. Describe your looks, your physical and mental health, your weight, your personality traits, etc. Be generous!

Gratitude Journal

Today I am thankful for…

Day 216:

I deserve enough time to rest.

When we don't sleep enough, our body and mind can't function optimally. Most people need to sleep 7 to 9 hours per day. How many hours do *you* need? <u>When should you go to bed and stand up</u> in order to give yourself enough time to rest every night? Make sure there is at least 7.5 hours between bedtime and the time you wake up.

Gratitude Journal

Today I am thankful for…

Day 217:

I'm showered with opportunities.

Close your eyes. Imagine a silver storm cloud over your head. It's a beautiful cloud, not menacing at all. Open your arms with your palms up and wait for the rain to start. Catch as many drops as you can. Imagine the silver drops are new opportunities. Hug them and put them in your heart. What do these silver drops contain?

Gratitude Journal

Today I am thankful for…

Day 218:

I fight for what I think is right.

Imagine you had enough time and money to join any cause of your choice tomorrow. Maybe volunteering at your kids' school, serving food to the homeless, or participating in environmental actions. What would be your cause of choice?

Gratitude Journal

Today I am thankful for…

Day 219:

I take good care of myself.

You probably take good care of others already. Now think about three things you can do this week to take better care of *yourself*.

1.
2.
3.

Gratitude Journal

Today I am thankful for…

Day 220:

I have enough material abundance for me and those who surround me.

Even if you have very little material things, you have got this book, pen and paper, so you probably have at least two or three things you could spare and donate. Make a list of things you could donate to share your abundance with others.

Gratitude Journal

Today I am thankful for…

Day 221:

I manifest miracles every day

Think about a miracle which could happen to you. Describe it in one sentence. Then shorten this sentence to one only word. Write this word somewhere you can see it every day. For example, if your word is *"house"*, write it on a post-it and stick it next to your computer screen or on the bathroom mirror. Every time you see it, say to yourself: *"thank you for…"* and add the word you chose.

Gratitude Journal

Today I am thankful for…

Day 222:

I believe in a better tomorrow.

If you can make every day a small percentage better and more successful than the one before, you will be on your way to a bright future. Plan your next week in advance. Think about one small thing you can do each day to make the week slightly better than the previous one.

Gratitude Journal

Today I am thankful for…

_____
_____
_____
_____

Day 223:

I enjoy great moments of intimacy.

Aphrodite is the Goddess of love and desire. With her help, try to picture the physical side of your ideal relationships. Afterwards, write the following affirmation: ***"I deserve and enjoy great moments of intimacy in my life."*** You can change the sentence so that it fits your manifestation.

Gratitude Journal

Today I am thankful for…

Day 224:

I make evidence-based decisions.

Is there a decision you should make in the future? Try to do some research and gather information on the subject. Then make a list of advantages and disadvantages.

Gratitude Journal

Today I am thankful for…

Day 225:

I welcome change.

Are you afraid of change? If you are, how will you attract better and new things into your life? Write down at least three reasons why change should be welcome and not feared.

Gratitude Journal

Today I am thankful for…

Day 226:

I work hard and my efforts are rewarded.

Write about ways your current efforts are going to be rewarded. Avoid expressions such as "*I hope*", "*I want*", "*I need*". ***"The effort I have put in… is about to be rewarded in this way…"***

Gratitude Journal

Today I am thankful for…

Day 227:

I trust others to do what I can't do myself.

Write about things you could start delegating from today on. They can be things at work, but your list could also include mundane but necessary things such as taking out the trash, walking the dog, vacuuming, etc. Who could do a few things instead of you? If you are overburdened, don't be ashamed to ask for help.

Gratitude Journal

Today I am thankful for…

Day 228:

Art is one of my healers.

What is your favorite form of art? Why? Does it have a place in your life already? How?

Gratitude Journal

Today I am thankful for…

Day 229:

I see beauty in everything.

Today, pick two mundane tasks you do every day: cleaning, walking to work, anything. Then think about ways this tasks can be made more beautiful.

Gratitude Journal

Today I am thankful for…

Day 230:

I see beauty in everyone.

Pick two acquaintances or famous people you don't like much. Now make an effort to say three good things about each of them.

Gratitude Journal

Today I am thankful for…

Day 231:

My intuition speaks to me clearly.

Ask your inner voice now. Of all your future plans, which one should you focus on first?

Gratitude Journal

Today I am thankful for…

Day 232:

I know when it's time to wait.

Just like yesterday, connect with your intuition first. Ask your inner voice: ***"which of my future plans should wait now because it's not ripe enough?"***

Gratitude Journal
Today I am thankful for…

Day 233:

There are things I can do better than anyone else.

Write about those things you excel at.

Gratitude Journal

Today I am thankful for…

Day 234:

I know when to say no.

Finish these sentences:
"No, I won't..."
"No, I don't want to..."
"No, I don't have time for..."

Gratitude Journal

Today I am thankful for…

Day 235:

Endings bring new beginnings.

Write about something that ended lately. It can be a course, a relationship, a book, a job, a friendship, anything. Think about good things which could arise from that ending.

Gratitude Journal

Today I am thankful for…

Day 236:

I am a fighter.

Make a list of things which are worth fighting for (of course you can fight for them in peaceful ways, too).

Gratitude Journal

Today I am thankful for…

Day 237:

Unhealthy relationships and people have no space in my life.

Draw a box. Write inside the box the names of those who deserve a space in your life. You can write outside those who haven't earned a place in your box yet, or leave the outside space blank. Remember people can earn a place in the box later.

Gratitude Journal

Today I am thankful for…

_____

_____

_____

_____

Day 238:

I am smart.

You are smart. Only smart people take time to work on themselves. Finish this sentence: ***"I am smart, because…"***

Gratitude Journal

Today I am thankful for…

Day 239:

I am self-confident.

Finish the sentences:

I know I'm on the right path because...

I love my body and my personality because...

Gratitude Journal

Today I am thankful for...

Day 240:

I learn from my mistakes.

Write about a mistake you made (big or small) which ended up being a great school of life:

Gratitude Journal

Today I am thankful for…

Day 241:

I am stronger than I look.

Some people may look weak, clumsy or small at first sight, but they hide an incredible inner strength and unbelievable capabilities. Why are *you* stronger than you look?

Gratitude Journal

Today I am thankful for…

Day 242:

Art helps me discover my inner self.

Write or draw freely. Let your hands choose what they want to do. If you just want to scribble, do it. You can also draw mindlessly, like you do when we are on the phone.

Gratitude Journal

Today I am thankful for…

Day 243:

I am proud of my body.

Write at least three things you love about your body. Please don't write there is nothing, because everybody has dozens of good qualities, whether they are aware of them or not.

Gratitude Journal

Today I am thankful for…

FIFTH JOURNALING CYCLE

Goddess Hestia

Hestia is the Greek Goddess of the hearth, home and family. For the ancient Greek it was of utmost importance to keep the fireplace burning, both from a spiritual and a practical point of view. The hearth was used for cooking, heating and ritual. In a time without lighters or electricity, keeping the hearth alive was vital, and Hestia's role was a very important one, despite its simplicity and possible monotony. Hestia was usually depicted as a modest, middle-aged and peaceful housewife who dedicated her life to tend to the hearth and to take care of the house and family. She was the third virgin Goddess, although very different in her character from the exuberant Artemis and Athena.

Hestia's story

Hestia is known as *Vesta* in Roman mythology. She became a virgin Goddess by choice, because the Gods of the Olympus were fighting to decide who would marry her. Hestia loved peace, so in order to put an end to the escalating conflict, she decided to choose none of her suitors. She made a vow to remain chaste and unmarried forever. After that, Zeus, the King of the Gods, awarded her the central place in each home, right by the hearth, and gave her the task to take care of the burning fire of the home for all eternity.

Hestia's symbols

Hestia's main symbol is the hearth, which is the heart and soul of the home. The first offering when moving into a new home was always made to Hestia.

How Hestia can help you

Hestia is a Goddess of peace and modesty. She works in the background, but her job is of utmost importance. Hestia's archetype is that of many modern-day housewives (or homemakers), who stay at home and forgo their own personal success in business in order to make sure everyone in the family is taken care of. They put the home in order, drive children to doctors' appointments and make sure there is always food in the house. They are the invisible pillars of our societies. Without Hestia, and her human equivalents, there couldn't be peace, warmth and love in the home. There couldn't be a home at all.

Even if you are not interested in marrying or having children, Hestia's energy is the one which warms up the place and turns a house into a home. She brings peace from the inside, comfort and satisfaction in life.

Day 244:

I feel supported.

Write your name in a box. Under this box, write the names of all those who support you in your endeavors. If someone hasn't come into your life yet, or isn't supporting you yet, write a placeholder such as *"partner"*, *"loving mother"*, etc.

Gratitude Journal

Today I am thankful for…

Day 245:

I am healthier and stronger every day.

Write about your ideal state of health. Use the present tense. Don't write *"I would like to have less pain in my wrists"*. It is much more effective to write something like this: *"I am thankful for my wrists, because they feel great and strong and I can type painlessly for hours on end"*.

Gratitude Journal

Today I am thankful for…

Day 246:

I live in my ideal home.

Before you manifest your ideal home, you need to know what it looks like! Draw your ideal home. You can browse real estate ads for ideas.

THIS IS MY HOME.

Gratitude Journal

Today I am thankful for…

Day 247:

I love my neighborhood.

Where is the future house of your dreams located? Be specific: country, city, and neighborhood. You can even write the street name and number if you know it.

Gratitude Journal

Today I am thankful for…

Day 248:

My life is a contribution to future generations.

Living fully today is a step towards leaving a useful legacy behind. Think about your future grandchildren, the grandchildren of those you love and those you will never get to know: what can you do for them today?

Gratitude Journal

Today I am thankful for…

Day 249:

I can solve any problem on my own.

You are able to solve any problem on your own if you have to. Try to remember about a time when you were proud of yourself for doing something difficult on your own.

Gratitude Journal

Today I am thankful for…

Day 250:

I can create my reality.

- 250 days of journaling. How are you going to celebrate?
- Draw or describe yourself in each of the squares below:

Past	Present	Future

Gratitude Journal

Today I am thankful for…

_____
_____
_____
_____
_____

Day 251:

I have made peace with my past.

Write about making peace with the least pleasant memories from your past. You can say good-bye to them, or thank them for the learning experience. Making peace with the past is necessary to achieve a brighter future.

Gratitude Journal

Today I am thankful for…

Day 252:

I deserve wealth.

Describe your future wealth as if you already possessed it. Remember to be thankful. Who will you share your wealth with?

Gratitude Journal

Today I am thankful for…

Day 253:

The Universe guides me.

You are guided and heard. Take some time to write a prayer today. It doesn't have to be a standard one, use your own style and beliefs.

Gratitude Journal

Today I am thankful for…

Day 254:

My home has a heart.

Who or what is the heart of your home? What makes your home something more than a roofed brick structure? Is it you? Is it something or someone else?

Gratitude Journal

Today I am thankful for…

Day 255:

The world is awaiting to meet my uniqueness.

Think about what makes you unique and how could it be useful for the world. Who can appreciate what you have to offer?

Gratitude Journal

Today I am thankful for…

Day 256:

I am surrounded by good friends.

Today, say thank you for your friends. For example: *"I am thankful to have (Michelle) in my life, because..."*

Gratitude Journal

Today I am thankful for…

Day 257:

I am bound to visit wonderful places.

Plan a trip to a place you have always dreamed to visit. When will you go? Who will go with you? Where and for how long will you stay? What will you do there?

Gratitude Journal

Today I am thankful for…

Day 258:

I handle daily life calmly and successfully.

Describe how you would react <u>calmly and elegantly</u> to small but annoying occurrences, such as: *Spilling your coffee / Being late to an appointment / Having someone stain your favorite clothes / Meeting an impatient driver on the road.*

Gratitude Journal

Today I am thankful for…

Day 259:

There is always someone ready to help me.

Write a list of people you would call in case you needed help, being thankful for their willingness to help with certain issues. For example: *"I am thankful for my mother because she helps babysit the children"*, *"I am thankful for Sharon because she answers my messages even if it's late"*.

Gratitude Journal

Today I am thankful for…

Day 260:

I make beautiful memories.

Today, imagine you can travel ten years into the future and look back. Write the future date and describe how this year you changed your life and what you did to achieve it. For example: *"December 21, 2035: ten years ago, I decided to start journaling, and then…"*

Gratitude Journal

Today I am thankful for…

Day 261:

I know the best way to say difficult things

Setting boundaries is great, but doing it kindly is even better. For example: *how could you start a kind conversation with your neighbor about their crying child waking you up every night? How would you tell your mother-in-law you really don't like her Christmas presents, and could she please stop buying you reindeer sweaters?* Think about ways you have tackled similar situations in the past, or write about the ones in the example.

Gratitude Journal

Today I am thankful for…

Day 262:

Family happiness is my birthright.

Draw a big heart, or a circle if you prefer. Then draw inside your ideal family, or their names/placeholders.

Gratitude Journal

Today I am thankful for…

Day 263:

I make time for spiritual practices.

What spiritual practices have you included (or would you like to include) in your daily routine?

Gratitude Journal

Today I am thankful for…

Day 264:

The power of the Goddesses supports my dreams.

Close your eyes and breathe slowly until you start to feel relaxed. Try to recall any of the Goddesses you have met in this journal. When one of them appears in your mind, ask her for a positive message regarding your dreams and expectations. Write down whatever encouraging messages come up.

Gratitude Journal

Today I am thankful for…

Day 265:

Bad habits have no power over me anymore.

Write about at least one bad habit you have managed to get rid of. It can be something small, like biting your nails, or something much harder. You can also write about bad habits you are still trying to tame. In this case, write as if you had abandoned them already, for example: *"I'm proud of myself for quitting smoking"*.

Gratitude Journal

Today I am thankful for…

Day 266:

I belong to a peaceful family.

Write about peaceful and harmonious family relationships (partner, parents, siblings, children, etc.). If your family relationships are already great, say thank you for what you have. If they aren't yet, write as if they were so, in order to manifest the changes you desire.

Gratitude Journal

Today I am thankful for…

Day 267:

I am not afraid of speaking aloud.

We all feel the need to keep silent sometimes. We do it to preserve the family peace, to keep a job, to avoid exposing ourselves … does it sound familiar? Is there anything you would like to say aloud, but you don't, for similar reasons? Write about it and visualize yourself speaking aloud about the subject, even if you can't do it in real life yet.

Gratitude Journal

Today I am thankful for…

Day 268:

I am deaf and blind to negativity.

Don't let negative people discourage you. It can be hard to stay positive 24/7, and even harder when others try to dishearten you. Today, build a negativity shield around you. Draw yourself in the rectangle below. Then draw a circle around yourself. Make it as thick as necessary, or use color markers. This is your negativity shield, and nobody can cross it without your permission. From now on, as long as you have your shield on, no negativity will be able to reach you.

Gratitude Journal

Today I am thankful for…

Day 269:

I have genius ideas.

Great ideas don't usually come to life fully formed. Make a habit to write down or sketch your ideas as soon as they come to mind. Is there an idea, an invention, a business plan, something which has been forming in your mind lately? Get it out of your head. Write about it in a rough draft, or draw it. Is it about selling, building, inventing something? Don't worry if it seems silly, or impossible: once you put it to paper you can start improving it.

Gratitude Journal

Today I am thankful for…

Day 270:

I always choose wisely.

Choices can be overwhelming. Should I do this? Should I get that? Should I get rid of this? Write about a choice you need to make. Then write the best possible outcome for each possibility.

	What?	Best possible outcome:
1		
2		

Gratitude Journal

Today I am thankful for…

Day 271:

I recognize hopeless situations and move on.

Make a list of situations which look like dead ends right now.

Gratitude Journal

Today I am thankful for…

Day 272:

I see the good side of every situation.

Today, think about a negative situation in your life and try to find one or more good things about it. Even things like pain remind us that we are still alive, that we are survivors and worth of admiration.

Gratitude Journal

Today I am thankful for…

Day 273:

I am forgiven.

Whatever you did in the past, it's in the past now. Think about ways you could make your wrongs right. If it isn't possible anymore, forgive yourself. ***"Today, I forgive myself for… and I love myself unconditionally."***

Gratitude Journal

Today I am thankful for…

Day 274:

I am my best friend.

Are you friends with yourself? Do you like yourself? Hopefully you do! Write a letter to yourself like you were your best friend. Include your best wishes. For example: *"Dear Anne, how are you? I have missed you so much. I hope your mother is getting better and your paintings are selling well…"*

Gratitude Journal

Today I am thankful for…

Day 275:

I am healing.

Draw yourself and color your body lovingly. Remind yourself that your body can and is healing. Write **"*I am healing*"** next to each part of your body which needs attention.

Gratitude Journal

Today I am thankful for…

_____
_____
_____
_____
_____

Day 276:

I am independent.

"I am independent, because…"

Gratitude Journal

Today I am thankful for…

Day 277:

I am loved.

Write about situations (past or future) which show how you are loved by others.

Gratitude Journal

Today I am thankful for…

Day 278:

I am a winner.

Describe yourself achieving victory in a situation (past or future).

Gratitude Journal

Today I am thankful for…

Day 279:

The Universe won't assign me any mission I can't deal with.

Do you ever feel overwhelmed by the assignments life puts on your shoulders? Choose one of them. Write down how you will successfully complete your mission.

Gratitude Journal

Today I am thankful for…

Day 280:

My true self deserves to be seen and heard.

Imagine the newspaper were to write about you and your achievements in one year's time. Write the headlines and a small article about yourself, dated next year.

NEWS

Gratitude Journal

Today I am thankful for…

Day 281:

I am authoritative.

Write down some firm orders for someone or *something*. Take advantage of the occasion! You can even try giving orders to rebellious inanimate objects like a car which doesn't want to start on cold mornings, the weather, or a computer who tends to freeze too often. Practice your authority in a fun way so you can use it later in real life.

Gratitude Journal

Today I am thankful for…

Day 282:

I am calm and peaceful.

A great way of calming stress is continuous-line drawing. Draw anything you want, it doesn't matter if it's just a shapeless doodle. The only rule is not to lift the pencil from the paper until you finish. Grade your stress level from 1 to 10 before you start. Do this exercise for a while and grade your levels again. If you find it helps you, you can use this technique whenever you want to: it's very simple and discrete.

Gratitude Journal

Today I am thankful for…

Day 283:

I am at peace.

Describe a peaceful day and night in your ideal life. Don't forget to include how peaceful and secure you feel inside.

Gratitude Journal

Today I am thankful for…

Day 284:

I know who I am.

If you had to describe yourself with only one or two words, what would it be? *Mother? Teacher? Engineer? Happy?* Who or what are you? Use a neutral or positive word.

Gratitude Journal

Today I am thankful for…

Day 285:

I believe in small good deeds.

Think about small good deeds you could do from time to time to make others happy with little effort.

Gratitude Journal

Today I am thankful for…

Day 286:

Suffering is in the past now.

Write a good-bye letter to everything which made you suffer in the past. Tell those things thank you for the lessons learned and farewell.

Gratitude Journal

Today I am thankful for…

Day 287:

I am kind.

Breathe deeply. Smile. Keep smiling. Think about someone (or something) who deserves your kindness. Write a small thank you note for them. Try not to stop smiling until you finish writing. Feel the thankfulness. Does it make you feel better?

Gratitude Journal

Today I am thankful for…

Day 288:

I am truthful.

Truthful is one level more advanced than *honest*. If being *honest* means *not lying*, being *truthful* means *telling the truth*. Did you tell any small lies lately? Maybe someone asked you why you were late, or whether you liked their new dress. Take some time and find a way you could have been truthful without being offensive.

Gratitude Journal

Today I am thankful for…

Day 289:

Lady Luck is smiling at me.

What would be the first thing you would do if you were completely sure *Lady Luck* was smiling at you?

Gratitude Journal

Today I am thankful for…

Day 290:

I build my dreams, one brick at a time.

The bricks below represent your goals and dreams. Write a goal on each brick. The first ones are below and create a foundation for the later ones. You don't have to fill in all the blanks if you don't want to.

Gratitude Journal

Today I am thankful for…

Day 291:

I embrace my spiritual side.

How do you bring spirituality into your life? Do you attend a temple, practice breathing, meditation, prayer, chanting…? Is there anything you would like to add to your life but you still haven't?

Gratitude Journal

Today I am thankful for…

Day 292:

I enjoy childlike happiness.

Make a list of things which make you feel happy and carefree. Maybe it's dancing, talking to certain people or watching certain movies or soap operas. Find out what brings out the happy child who sleeps inside of you, and then make time to do a few of those things during the week.

Gratitude Journal

Today I am thankful for…

Day 293:

Life is my teacher.

Remember when you were at school? Did you ever raise your hand to ask what you didn't understand, or were you one of those who preferred to hide in the back row? Today you are in a completely different classroom and your teacher is *Mrs. Life*. Raise your hand and pose any questions you have for her. Don't be shy. You are going to get all straight A's this time.

Gratitude Journal

Today I am thankful for…

Day 294:

I am a survivor.

Complete this sentence: *"I am a survivor, because of… and I am thankful for all the past experiences, which taught me…"*

Gratitude Journal

Today I am thankful for…

Day 295:

I have a loving family.

Today is the last day in Hestia's cycle. Say thank you once more for your loving family, whoever they are.

Gratitude Journal

Today I am thankful for…

SIXTH JOURNALING CYCLE

Goddess Demeter

You reap what you sow.

Demeter is the Greek Goddess of the harvest. We have arrived to the sixth and last journaling cycle and now it's time to finish shaping the goals you wish to manifest and start reaping the benefits. This journal started with Persephone, Demeter's daughter and Queen of the Underworld, and it ends with her mother, who makes the land fertile and helps all living creatures grow and ripen on the Earth.

Demeter's story

Demeter was in charge of the fertility of the Earth. When her daughter Persephone was abducted by Hades and taken to the Underworld, Demeter became so sad and angry that she let the land become completely barren. The Gods were so worried about the consequences of Demeter's grief that they managed to make an agreement with Hades so that Persephone and her mother could be reunited for at least a few months every year.

Mortals honor Demeter as her good will brings the harvest every year. She makes crops grow and is in charge of the cycles of life and death.

In Roman Mythology Demeter is known as *Ceres*.

Demeter's symbols

Demeter's symbols include: a cornucopia full of fruits and cereals, wheat and other cereal grains and spikes, and a torch to search for Persephone in the darkness of the Underworld.

How Demeter can help you

Fill the cornucopia of your life with abundance and shape a better future for yourself during the next journaling weeks. Afterwards, you may be ready to start a new and deeper cycle of journaling and self-exploration with Persephone.

Day 296:

The most fertile period of my life just started.

What area of your life needs to become the most fertile right now? You needn't use the term *fertility* literally, as in *having children*. Creativity and imagination can be fertile, too. Abundance and growth can be wished for in many areas of life.

Gratitude Journal

Today I am thankful for…

Day 297:

I banish useless worrying.

Throw into the trash bin any thoughts, items (and maybe *people?*) which need to be binned right now. You can leave things by the bin, if there isn't enough space inside. Don't worry, the Universe's garbage truck is around the corner and will pick everything up.

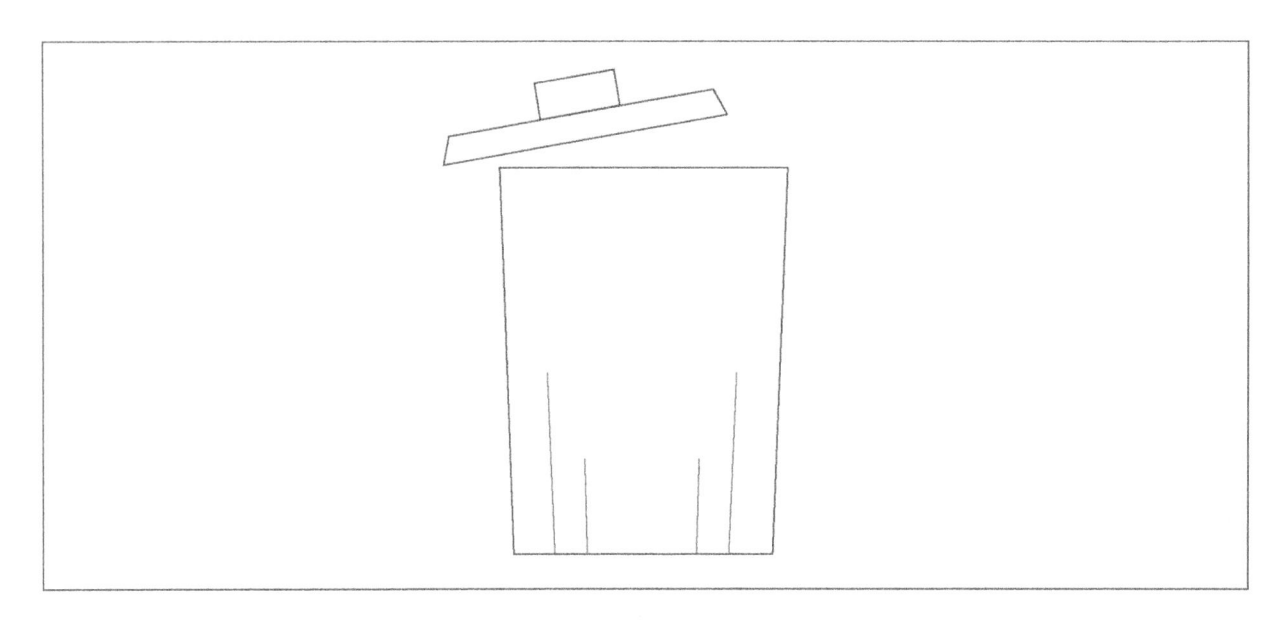

Gratitude Journal

Today I am thankful for…

Day 298:

I am ready now to show myself to the world.

Write a few reasons why you believe in yourself and your potential.

Gratitude Journal

Today I am thankful for…

Day 299:

Optimism is my way of life.

Write down two or three optimistic thoughts. If you can't think of any, do it the opposite way: reflect about all those things you have negative or pessimistic thoughts about and write the opposite. Example: if you keep thinking they are not going to call you for that job interview, you can write: *"I'm sure they are going to call me for that job interview."*

Gratitude Journal

Today I am thankful for…

Day 300:

I am an achiever.

You earned some free-style journaling to celebrate your 300th journaling session. Decide how you are going to reward yourself.

Gratitude Journal

Today I am thankful for…

Day 301:

I turn to those who know more for advice.

Think about areas of your life where you feel stuck. Then try to find out who could help you out.

Gratitude Journal

Today I am thankful for…

Day 302:

Justice will turn in my favor.

If you are waiting for the scales of justice to balance in any area of life, write down the outcome as it had already happened. Visualize how it will happen in as much detail as possible. Say thank you for the favorable outcome.

Gratitude Journal

Today I am thankful for…

Day 303:

I choose wisely who I spend time with.

Have you ever spent some time talking to someone, just to feel completely exhausted afterwards? Try to make a list of reasons why this happens. Write about the traits such people have in common.

Gratitude Journal

Today I am thankful for…

Day 304:

I am enough.

Repeat it as many times as you need: ***I am enough***. There might be people around you who constantly remind you of all your faults and the things you did wrong. Some people simply can't do better: they can't perceive their own worth unless they devalue others. But that's their problem, not yours. If you have such people around you, write down this affirmation until you believe it: ***Thank you. I love you. I am enough.***

Gratitude Journal

Today I am thankful for…

Day 305:

I enjoy moments of solitude.

Make a plan for the next time you get to spend time alone. What would you like to do? Maybe reading, painting, going for a walk? Resting or sleeping is also fine. It's a good habit to make plans with yourself from time to time.

Gratitude Journal

Today I am thankful for…

Day 306:

Everything in moderation.

Make a list of things where you could exercise moderation.

Gratitude Journal

Today I am thankful for…

Day 307:

Lies and duplicity don't affect me.

Imagine past moments when you were lied to or cheated on. Imagine the outcome of the situation turning in your favor. Finish the sentence: ***"Lies and duplicity don't affect me anymore, because…"***

Gratitude Journal

Today I am thankful for…

Day 308:

I reap love and abundance.

You have been sowing love and abundance for months. Now it's time you reap the benefits. Write on each wheat spike what you are going to harvest:

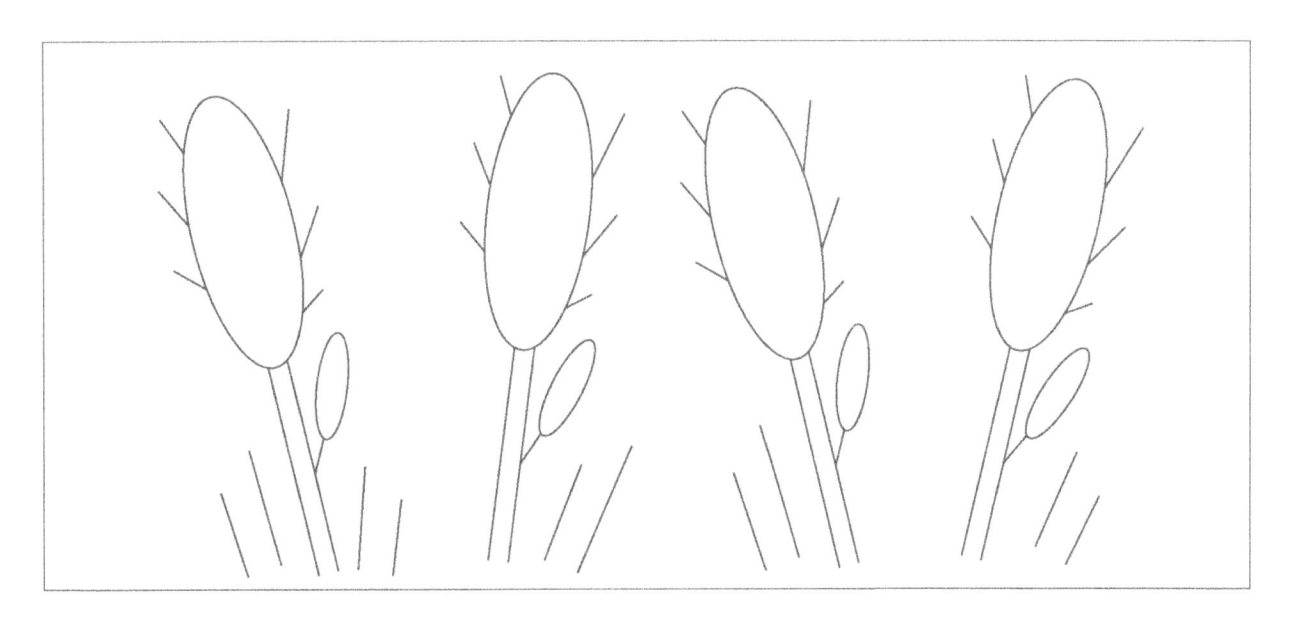

Gratitude Journal

Today I am thankful for…

_____
_____
_____
_____
_____

Day 309:

I trust my inner compass.

What is your next stop? What project should you tackle first? What does your inner compass tell you?

Gratitude Journal

Today I am thankful for…

Day 310:

I have a fertile imagination.

Imagination is great because it helps you find creative ways to solve problems. Let your imagination loose and do some automatic writing. Just write anything which comes to your mind. If you are afraid of blank pages, start with: *"I don't know what to write, but..."*

Gratitude Journal

Today I am thankful for…

Day 311:

My life is an oasis of peace.

Imagine what your life would look like if all conflicts were resolved and all stress gone. Describe it as if it were happening right now, for example: *"I'm so happy my relationship with (Hannah) is finally harmonious…"*

Gratitude Journal

Today I am thankful for…

Day 312:

I deserve love.

If you ever felt you were not worthy of true love, it's about time you erase that thought from your mind. You deserve to be loved and appreciated. Write at least three reasons why. For example: "*I deserve to be loved, because (I am honest).*"

Gratitude Journal

Today I am thankful for…

Day 313:

I love myself.

Do you love yourself more than anyone else? You should. They say you can't pour from an empty cup. Write down a few loving words to fill your personal love cup. For example: *"I am hardworking; I am beautiful..."*

Gratitude Journal

Today I am thankful for…

Day 314:

I am able to make myself and others happy.

Think about one or two things you could do in the coming days or week to make someone else happy.

Gratitude Journal

Today I am thankful for…

Day 315:

I feel safe.

Do you feel safe? Feeling unsafe or unsure is more common than it seems, and given the world we live in, it's not surprising at all. Still, <u>you need to have a safe space and safe people in your life</u> so your system can relax. Who (or what) is your safe haven? If you don't have one yet, imagine it and describe it.

Gratitude Journal

Today I am thankful for…

Day 316:

I am able to forgive.

If you can, send love to those who wronged you. You can write: ***"Even though I don't understand why you (did that), I send you love and forgive you, so I can be free."***

Gratitude Journal

Today I am thankful for…

Day 317:

I delegate what I can't do myself.

Think about any responsibilities you could delegate to others. Maybe you need a secretary, a nanny or a dog-walker, but can't afford them yet. In that case, manifest them with an affirmation like this: *"I'm so thankful for the new, loving nanny who is about to come into my life and help me take care of my children."*

Gratitude Journal

Today I am thankful for…

Day 318:

My mind is clear.

Mind-decluttering is an ongoing process. Just like showering, it must be repeated often so that it works properly. Do some mental decluttering now and take a few minutes to realize what the really important thoughts are.

Gratitude Journal

Today I am thankful for…

Day 319:

I leave a beautiful legacy behind.

How do you want to be remembered in one or two hundred years? *"Michelle was a great dentist, she always took time to talk to each patient and help them with their pain."* Think about your mission on Earth.

Gratitude Journal

Today I am thankful for…

Day 320:

I rest when I need it.

A well-rested body and mind are crucial in order to achieve your goals. What activities help you relax? Meditation? Yoga? Going to the gym? Walking the dogs? Make a list of activities which help you relax your body and/or mind, and promise yourself to add at least two of them to your weekly plans.

Gratitude Journal

Today I am thankful for…

Day 321:

I share my abundance with those who are less fortunate.

Find ways of sharing the abundance you already possess with those who need you. Make plans for sharing later, too, when you manifest your ideal state of abundance.

Gratitude Journal

Today I am thankful for…

Day 322:

I have everything I need to create the life of my dreams.

Imagine there was a recipe for creating the life of your dreams. Write down an *ingredient list*. Send your "order" to the Universe and have faith it will get *shipped* soon.

Your Order for the Universe:

_____
_____
_____
_____
_____
_____
_____

Order now?

☐ YES ☐ NO

Gratitude Journal

Today I am thankful for…

_____
_____
_____
_____

Day 323:

I have faith in a better future.

What exactly is a better future for you? Describe it.

Gratitude Journal

Today I am thankful for…

Day 324:

I leave behind what doesn't serve me.

Find at least one thing in your life you need to get rid of. Thank it and let it go.

Gratitude Journal

Today I am thankful for…

Day 325:

I am a Goddess in my own home.

Think about things you could do today or during the following days to make yourself feel more like a Goddess. Maybe a relaxing bath, a hair mask or a healthy smoothie. Make a list of things which make you feel healthy, relaxed and beautiful.

Gratitude Journal

Today I am thankful for…

Day 326:

Love is the answer.

Think about conflictive relationships in your life. Find ways to solve them in a loving way.

Gratitude Journal

Today I am thankful for…

Day 327:

I speak my truth.

Write down a truth you need to get out of your chest. You can erase it afterwards if you don't feel comfortable leaving it on paper.

___

Gratitude Journal

Today I am thankful for…

___

Day 328:

I am always helpful.

Is there anyone out there who needs your help right now?

Gratitude Journal

Today I am thankful for…

Day 329:

I always reach my goals.

Think about at least one goal you have achieved during the last year.

Gratitude Journal
Today I am thankful for…

Day 330:

I manifest great changes for those I love.

If you could make a wish for someone dear to you, what would it be? Write about the things you would like to manifest for your loved ones. *"I am thankful for (my sister passing all her exams in June), **if she accepts this manifestation.**"*

Gratitude Journal

Today I am thankful for…

Day 331:

I'm so thankful everything is going great for my loved ones.

Say thank you for the great things which are going to happen to your loved ones in the near future. You can use yesterday's wishes: *"I'm thankful Hellen is going to pass her exams, because she will be able to go to university next year as she wanted."*

Gratitude Journal

Today I am thankful for…

Day 332:

I manifest great changes in my community.

Think about your community, the people who surround you and the places you visit often: these are for example the parents of other schoolchildren, people from your same neighborhood, etc. What would you want to manifest for them and the places you frequent?

Gratitude Journal

Today I am thankful for…

Day 333:

I'm so thankful for the great things going on in my community.

Say thank you for the changes you manifested yesterday. For example: *"I'm so thankful for the new library in my town, because my neighbors and I will be able to read many books for free."*

Gratitude Journal

Today I am thankful for…

Day 334:

I manifest traveling to exciting new places.

Where would you like to go? Make a detailed list, writing down the travel dates, the destination and who is going with you.

Gratitude Journal

Today I am thankful for…

Day 335:

I am thankful for all the wonderful places I will visit.

Say thank you for your future travels, saying why they make you so happy. For example: *"I'm so happy I'm going to Athens next September, because I will finally get to see the Parthenon and feel Athena's energy."*

Gratitude Journal

Today I am thankful for…

Day 336:

I manifest enough free time to rest and enjoy myself.

How would it feel to have enough time every day to rest, read, or dedicate to your hobbies and your friends? How much time would you need? What would you do with that time? Complete the sentence: ***"I manifest … hours per day/week, and I am going to use them to…"***

Gratitude Journal

Today I am thankful for…

Day 337:

I am thankful for all the free time I have to enjoy life.

Write a thank-you note where you acknowledge all the wonderful free time you are going to manifest. Write in the present tense. *"I am so thankful to have one hour of free time each day, because…"*

Gratitude Journal

Today I am thankful for…

Day 338:

I manifest great friendships.

"I manifest (two fun and understanding friends who like to play chess like me), with whom I will be able to share…"

Gratitude Journal

Today I am thankful for…

Day 339:

I am thankful for all my good friends.

Say thank you for all the friends you (will) have and their unconditional support. *"I am thankful for having so many good friends around me, because they..."*

Gratitude Journal

Today I am thankful for...

Day 340:

I manifest the love and intimacy I always wanted in my life.

Describe the traits of your perfect partner. If you are already in a relationship with this person, congratulations! You can still add a few details which could be bettered. Or just say thanks for what you have. If you are alone and you like it that way, you can also be thankful for that.

Gratitude Journal

Today I am thankful for…

Day 341:

I am thankful for the love of my dreams.

Say thank you for the partner of your dreams and their personality. For example: *"I am so thankful for my partner, because he/she always finds time to listen to me when I'm worried without judging me."* Maybe it hasn't happened yet, but use the present tense anyway.

Gratitude Journal

Today I am thankful for...

Day 342:

I manifest my perfect family.

Who are the members of your ideal family, and how do they get along?

Gratitude Journal

Today I am thankful for…

Day 343:

I am thankful for my wonderful family.

Say thank you for all the wonderful things you have (or will have) in your ideal family. For example, you can write *"I am grateful for the peaceful and understanding relationship I have with my mother-in-law"*, even if you haven't achieved it yet.

Gratitude Journal

Today I am thankful for…

Day 344:

I live in the home of my dreams.

Describe the home of your dreams. Size, location, most important features… How do you feel living in there? How is it different from your current home?

Gratitude Journal

Today I am thankful for…

Day 345:

I am thankful for the home of my dreams.

Write a note saying thank you for the best features of your dream home. Write in the present tense, for example: *"I am thankful for the big and luminous kitchen in my new house, because now I have enough space to prepare and store healthy food for my family)*.

Gratitude Journal

Today I am thankful for…

Day 346:

I manifest financial abundance.

Imagine the financial abundance of your dreams. How much would you need in your bank account to feel comfortable? Write down the sum and how you would spend it, share it or invest it.

Gratitude Journal

Today I am thankful for…

Day 347:

I am thankful for all this financial abundance.

Write a thank you note to say thanks for all the financial abundance which is coming your way, starting today.

Gratitude Journal

Today I am thankful for…

Day 348:

I manifest perfect health.

Imagine your body and mind working perfectly. No ailments or pains. Visualize yourself dancing and enjoying your earthly body. What does it look like?

Gratitude Journal

Today I am thankful for…

Day 349:

I am thankful for my perfect health.

Write a thank-you note for the perfectly healthy body and mind you want to manifest.

Gratitude Journal

Today I am thankful for…

Day 350:

I am thankful for the wonderful days to come.

Now you have given shape to your manifestation, take a moment to write thank you for all the wonderful things in your near future.

Gratitude Journal

Today I am thankful for…

Day 351:

I am a Goddess and I rule in my Underworld.

To finish the last journaling cycle, we will pay a final visit to each of the Goddesses, starting with Persephone. Which of Persephone's talents do you possess already and which ones would you like to enhance with her help?

Gratitude Journal
Today I am thankful for…

Day 352:

I defeat my demons just like Persephone.

How can you use Persephone's example to enhance your life?

Gratitude Journal

Today I am thankful for…

Day 353:

I am a Goddess of feminity.

Which of Artemis's talents do you possess already and which ones would you like to enhance with her help?

Gratitude Journal

Today I am thankful for…

Day 354:

I am as wild and independent as Goddess Artemis.

How can you use Artemis's stories and energy to enhance your life?

Gratitude Journal

Today I am thankful for…

Day 355:

I am a Goddess of wisdom.

Which of Athena's talents do you possess already and which ones would you like to enhance with her help?

Gratitude Journal

Today I am thankful for…

Day 356:

I am as smart and brave as Goddess Athena.

How could you use Athena's energy to make your life better?

Gratitude Journal

Today I am thankful for…

Day 357:

I am a Goddess of beauty and love.

What qualities of Aphrodite do you possess already and which ones would you like to enhance with her help?

Gratitude Journal

Today I am thankful for…

Day 358:

I possess Aphrodite's beauty and allure.

How can you use Aphrodite's energy to enhance your life?

Gratitude Journal

Today I am thankful for…

Day 359:

I am the Goddess of my home and family.

What qualities of Goddess Hestia do you possess already, and which ones would you like to enhance?

Gratitude Journal

Today I am thankful for…

Day 360:

Hestia's fire will burn forever in my heart.

How can Hestia's influence help you in your life?

Gratitude Journal

Today I am thankful for…

Day 361:

I am a Goddess of fertility.

What qualities of Goddess Demeter do you possess already, and which ones would you like to enhance?

Gratitude Journal

Today I am thankful for…

Day 362:

Demeter helps me harvest all the good things I have sown.

How can Demeter's archetype help you?

Gratitude Journal

Today I am thankful for…

Day 363:

I am a Goddess.

Which of the Goddesses do you identify with the most? Which of them is the least similar to you?

Gratitude Journal

Today I am thankful for…

Day 364:

I am thankful for the great times ahead.

Say thank you for all the wonders you are about to manifest. Some of them might have started to make themselves tangible by now.

Gratitude Journal

Today I am thankful for…

Day 365:

I did it.

Congratulations! You finished this journal. You have been loyal to the promise you made to yourself one year ago. If you can do this, you can do anything. Has anything changed for the better since you started journaling? Are you ready to start the cycle again? Give yourself a reward for your hard work. Not everyone gets to this page, but you did it!

Gratitude Journal

Today I am thankful for…

About the Author

I was born by the Mediterranean Sea, and I took my first steps on the same land where ancient fertility Goddess Tanit was revered thousands of years ago. That same land was later treaded on by the Greek, as it became a Greek colony, and later by the Romans and many other conquerors after them. The Ancient Goddesses didn't disappear, though: they were worshipped by our ancestors by many other names. Goddess Tanit was syncretized with Greek Goddesses Aphrodite, Demeter and Artemis, whose myths are referred to in this journal. They later became Venus, Ceres and Diana. The Great Goddesses are still revered by many and remain great sources of inspiration and spiritual growth for anyone. I'd like to give endless thanks for the Goddesses' everlasting energy, which can still be felt in the sea breeze of the Ancient Carthage and its long lost colonies.

Thank you.

Other books by the same author:

- *The Solitary Witch's Green Book* (available as an eBook, paperback and audiobook)
- *The Solitary Witch's Green Journal*
- *Tarot Journal & Coloring Book*

Made in the USA
Monee, IL
18 December 2019